All About the Desert

By Sam and Beryl Epstein

Illustrated by Fritz Kredel

RANDOM HOUSE
NEW YORK

THIRD PRINTING

LIBRARY OF CONGRESS CATALOG CARD NUMBER: 57-7519
MANUFACTURED IN THE UNITED STATES OF AMERICA

Contents

Deserts Are Alike in Only One Way

The deserts of the world are not all alike.

Some of them are large; some are fairly small. The famous Painted Desert in Arizona is about the size of the state of Connecticut. The vast Sahara, which covers most of northern Africa, is as big as the whole United States.

Some deserts lie almost at sea level, and at certain places they dip below that point. Some are on high plateaus. Some rise and fall like rolling farm land. Whole mountain ranges cut through certain deserts, dividing them into sections as the walls of a house divide it into rooms. Sometimes a desert ends abruptly. Sometimes it blends so gradually into some other kind of land that even experts can't say exactly where the desert's boundary is.

All About the Desert

Not all the world's desert areas look alike either. In only a few of them could you see the wind-drifted dunes that so many people think of when they talk about deserts. Even the various sections of a single desert look quite different from each other. One part may be floored with hard-packed sand, another part with gravel or loose rock, still another part with flat stones so neatly set in place that they seem to be a carefully laid pavement.

Plants differ, too, from one desert to another. The cactus is very much a part of the scenery in most of the desert country of Mexico and our own Southwest. Arizona is so proud of its tall treelike saguaro cactus that it has chosen the creamy saguaro blossom as its official state flower. But there are no cacti at all in the great Gobi that stretches halfway across Asia. And the only cacti that grow in the deserts of Africa and Arabia, or in the great deserts of Australia, are plants that were imported from the Western Hemisphere.

The animals of one desert also differ from those that live in another. We would be surprised to see a camel wandering through California's Mojave Desert today, even though camels did live there in prehistoric times. But camel caravans are common in the Sahara, the

In American deserts you often see tall saguaro cactus and the cocky little road runner.

Arabian deserts and the Gobi. The ostrich, a familiar sight to the natives of Africa's Kalahari Desert, would be a stranger in South America's desert, that long barren stretch of country in Chile known as the Atacama. An ostrich would also look odd loping along beside the road runner, the sturdy, cocky little bird that is so much at home in our American deserts.

But in spite of all these differences, all deserts are alike in one very important way. They all have a scarcity of the kind of water that most land plants and animals need.

This doesn't mean that all deserts are dry, like America's deserts of the Southwest and the other deserts that have already been mentioned.

The land north of the Arctic Circle, for example, is a kind of desert. It has plenty of water in the form of ice. But animals can't drink frozen water, and plants can't draw it up through their roots. So the regions of the Arctic and other very cold lands are deserts too. They are sometimes called "deserts of the cold."

An ocean or a salt-lake beach is another kind of desert. Rain may fall on it very often, and the tide may flow over it every day. It may even be flooded with water, but the water will all be salty. Even the fresh rain that falls on it becomes salty when it mixes with the salt-soaked beach sand. So, since most land plants and animals can't live on salty water, sandy beaches are also deserts of a special kind. They are sometimes called "deserts of the salt."

Still another kind of desert is a salt-water marsh. There too the water is all salty. That's why marshes at the edge of oceans or salt-water lakes are called "deserts of the wet."

But deserts, to most people, are those places where there is little water of any kind—not even frozen water or salt water. Scientists call them "dry deserts" to make sure they are not confused with deserts of other kinds.

In those deserts the earth is very dry and the air is dry too. Rain falls very seldom and only during one or two brief periods during the year.

These dry deserts, which together cover one-seventh of the land surface of the earth, are the deserts you will read about in this book. They are not all alike, and they are scattered around the world in every continent except Europe. These deserts have just that one thing in common. They all have a scarcity of water.

2

Getting Along on Very Little Water

The word *desert* comes from an old Latin word that means "deserted," and some desert areas are so dry that they are completely deserted so far as people are concerned. Others have a human population of one or two persons for each square mile. (In New Jersey the population is over 250 persons for each square mile.)

But most deserts have large populations of both plants and animals. They may not be very noticeable, because desert animals don't show themselves very often, especially in the daytime, and because desert plants usually grow rather far apart. But they are there and they are thriving. And though they are of many different kinds—large and small, short-lived and long-lived, handsome and ugly—they too are all alike in one way. The one quality they all share is the ability to get along on very little water.

Some do this by economizing on water, some by storing water, and some by manufacturing water.

Plants use the first two methods. Animals use all three, although only a few animals can use the third which is the most unusual system for surviving under desert conditions.

The Economizers

Desert plants and animals that economize on water are rather like people who have learned to live on a small income. They spend no more than the little money they receive. These desert plants and animals don't "spend" more water than they get. Some of them get less than others, of course, depending on where they live and what they live on. Those which get the least can stay alive only by spending the least. Some of them spend so little water that they deserve the name of water misers.

One remarkable water miser is a toad, a creature most people never think of as a desert dweller at all, because they know it must be born in the water and spend the first part of its life there. In fact, in most parts of the world baby toads or tadpoles spend several months in the water before their fishlike gills turn into lungs and they grow legs and come out on dry land.

A spadefoot toad gets moisture only from insects it eats.

But the spadefoot toad survives very well in the driest parts of the Sonoran Desert in Arizona. After a hard spring rain, when a few puddles form here and there in low areas, the female toads lay their eggs in those puddles. If the puddles dry up by the next day, the eggs don't get a chance to hatch. But if the puddles last even two days, they are suddenly full of tiny tadpoles. And if even a little water remains for just two weeks, these desert tadpoles are ready to live on land. Their gills have already changed into lungs, they have lost their tails, and their legs are grown.

From then on the only moisture the toads get comes from the insects they eat. Most of the time they hide away from the desert sun and heat in burrows dug with their hind legs. Sometimes they hide in their burrows for months at a time. Experts have said the spadefoots probably spend four-fifths of their lives lying motionless underground. By not moving, by not exposing themselves to sun and heat, they can economize on water to a remarkable degree.

Perhaps once a year, on the night after a big spring downpour, the spadefoots find a puddle and swim merrily about in it. That night they fill the quiet desert air with the sound of their noisy peeping. That night the female toads lay their eggs, and each year at least a few of those eggs hatch into a new generation of this strange toad-that-can-live-in-a-desert.

Many other desert animals hide away from the drying effects of desert climate just as the spadefoot does. They appear only at night and spend all the daylight hours in the shade of a bush or a stone, or in underground burrows. By lying low out of the hot sun, they economize on what little moisture they get.

All About the Desert

Desert plants, of course, can't hide during the day. That's why they have to economize on water in other ways.

The way they usually economize is not to spend water extravagantly through their leaves, as plants do in other parts of the world where it rains often. A lilac bush or an oak tree in Massachusetts or Virginia, for example, can afford to spread thousands of moist green leaves to the sunlight for many months of the year, even though they lose moisture through every leaf every day. If the lilac and the oak didn't get fresh water constantly through their roots, those leaves would dry up very quickly, just as wet clothes dry when they are spread in the hot sun.

Desert plants, which don't get a regular supply of water, wouldn't live very long if they spent water every day by letting a great deal of it evaporate from hundreds of leaf surfaces. That's why the leaves of some desert plants are turned so that only their edges, and not their moist flat surfaces, are exposed directly to hot drying sunlight. Other desert plant leaves are covered with a grayish fuzz that shades them from the light, or with a kind of wax or varnish coating that prevents their moisture from drying out. In many very dry desert areas the plants discard their leaves altogether for the greatest part of the year.

The ocotillo, sometimes called the coachwhip, looks like a cluster of bare slender whips stuck in the ground. It has no leaves at all except right after a rain. Then suddenly its stalks sprout hundreds of tiny green leaves. Just as suddenly, a few days or weeks later, those leaves drop off. The stalks are bare and dead-looking again until the next rain, which may not come for many months.

Like the leaves of all other plants, ocotillo leaves contain chlorophyll. That is the mysterious substance that uses sunlight as fuel and manufactures the building materials plants must have in order to grow. So the most remarkable thing about the ocotillo is that it survives even though it very seldom has chlorophyll-bearing leaves. The reason it can survive is that its stalks have a green bark which also contains chlorophyll. For most of the year that green bark does the work that leaves normally do for other plants. In fact, the ocotillo's bark does its work so well that every stalk of the plant can put forth a cluster of bright red flowers in April or May. Some people call it flaming sword or candlewood because those red flowers look rather like flames blazing brightly ten or fifteen feet above the desert floor.

The paloverde is another desert plant whose green bark can do the work that leaves usually do. Its name means "green stick," and for most of the year this shrub, or small tree, looks like nothing more than a bunch of branching green sticks. It has leaves only during the spring, when some rain usually falls in the Sonoran Desert of the American Southwest, where the paloverde thrives. The paloverde also blooms at that same period, and for a time it becomes a brilliant mass of small yellow or golden flowers. Indians used to grind the beanlike seed pods of this plant into a kind of flour.

The members of the fabulous cactus family are probably the best water economizers of all desert plants. They survive without ever having any leaves at all.

The prickly pear cactus, for example, looks as if it were made up of many flat, thick, spine-studded green leaves, stuck together, tip to tip. But these pads, called joints, are really the plant's stems. They contain all the chlorophyll the plant needs for the manufacture of its food. The wax coating on the pads prevents the moisture in them from evaporating rapidly. Thus the prickly pear can thrive in very dry areas.

Almost everyone who has ever visited our American

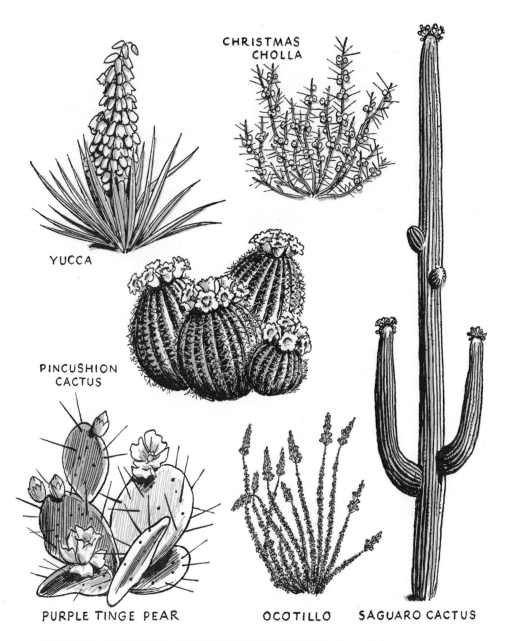

YUCCA

CHRISTMAS CHOLLA

PINCUSHION CACTUS

PURPLE TINGE PEAR

OCOTILLO

SAGUARO CACTUS

Plants of the desert have strange and wonderful shapes.

deserts knows the prickly pear. It is often seen growing in other parts of the country too. There are many varieties of it, some fairly small, some growing in large clumps. In the spring, lovely cup-shaped flowers bloom at the tips of the pads. Those flowers are yellow on the prickly pear most common in Texas and Arizona, and a dark red on the prickly pear most common in California. Later in the year large, juicy, purplish-red, pear-shaped fruits replace the flowers. The fruits are called tunas, and many people think they are delicious. Mexicans make a candy by straining and cooking the tuna juice. The candy looks and tastes rather like a piece of sweet potato.

The Water Storers

Most of the water storers in the desert are plants, but the desert tortoise and the camel also use this method of getting along on very little water.

Many tall tales have been told about the camel's ability to store water in its hump and to live for a long time without taking a drink. There is some truth in the stories, but they are not entirely true.

During the heat of a desert summer a camel must drink water every day. During the cooler desert winter

The desert tortoise gets all its water from a vegetable diet.

it can get along without water for months at a time. But even then it can do this only if it is getting plenty of good moist pasture and is not carrying heavy loads. And the camel doesn't store water in its hump at all, but in a small special compartment of the stomach. It is true that the camel can get along with so little water that it is the best pack animal for desert travel.

Not nearly so many stories have been told about the desert tortoise, but in one way it is much more remarkable than the camel. The tortoise never drinks at all. It gets all the water it needs from a juicy vegetable diet. In fact, after a rainfall when the desert plants are particularly juicy, the tortoise gets more water than it needs. That's when it stores water away in the two sacs, or bladders, tucked under its upper shell. The desert tortoise never grows very big. Usually it is less than a foot long. But apparently it can store as much as a pint of water at a time for use during dry periods when plants contain little moisture. Of course the tortoise economizes on water too, by moving very seldom and very slowly.

The most famous of the desert plant water storers is probably the barrel cactus. It really looks very like a spine-studded green barrel, and many people think of it as being full of water. They get this idea from stories they have heard about desert travelers, dying of thirst, who saved their lives by cutting off the top of a barrel cactus and drinking the liquid inside it.

But if you cut off the top of a barrel cactus, you find it filled with a white pulp which must be pounded in order to collect the cactus juice or water. People who have tasted this liquid say it is very bitter, and that they wouldn't drink it unless they really were dying of thirst. American Indians, for example, apparently never drank this "water" except in an emergency. But they are said to have used it in another way. They left it inside the cactus, added hot stones, and then boiled their meat in this handy natural cooking pot.

The barrel cactus stores up water after a rain when the ground is moist. Then its thousands of roots, spread out in a wide circle just under the surface of the ground, absorb a great deal of moisture which is quickly carried into the "barrel" above ground. The cylindrical wall of the barrel, creased into ridges all around like an accordion, stretches out to make room for the new supply of water. As the plant uses up its stored water supply, it shrinks again.

Because this plant often leans toward the south, many people have said it can be used as a guide through the desert. That's why it is sometimes called the compass cactus.

The night-blooming cereus can also store a great deal of water, but it stores its water underground in a huge turnip-like root that may weigh as much as fifty pounds. Above the ground this plant usually looks like a few dry dead sticks, perhaps six feet tall. If you walked past it, probably you would not notice it at all, unless you happened to pass on the night when its bare stalks burst into bloom. Then you would see one of the most spectacular sights of the desert. The great white flowers, which fill the air with their heavy scent, are so beautiful that the Mexicans have named this strange plant *Reina de la Noche*, which means "queen of the night."

The Water Manufacturers

One of the most interesting residents of our American deserts is a little fawn-colored mouselike member of the rodent family. It is called the kangaroo rat, although it is neither a rat nor a kangaroo. It gets its name from its unusually long hind legs, on which it leaps about the desert like a miniature kangaroo, holding its short front legs tucked up against its throat. It can leap a distance of ten feet, or approximately ten times its own length. Its tail, which is longer than the rest of its body, and tipped with a furry white brush, serves as a kind of rudder during these leaps. By twitching this tail the kangaroo rat can change direction in mid-air to avoid snakes and owls and larger desert animals that would like to make a meal of this curious little creature.

But the most remarkable thing about the kangaroo rat is that it can survive without ever tasting a drop of water. People who have made a pet of this friendly black-eyed animal have tried to persuade it to take a drink, but it never does. It doesn't even like to get its

By twitching its tail, the kangaroo rat can turn in mid-air.

silky fur wet, and during a rain it always stays inside the mazelike burrows where it makes its home. It doesn't eat a juicy diet either, as the non-drinking tortoise does. It lives on dry hard seeds, which it pushes into its cheek pouches with its tiny front feet and carries home to eat in safety.

All the water the kangaroo rat needs in order to keep alive—and it needs water just as every other living thing does—is produced in its own digestive system. This water-manufacturing process consists of combining the two elements of which water is made: hydrogen and oxygen. The kangaroo rat gets oxygen from the air it breathes, and hydrogen from those dry seeds it eats.

All About the Desert

Inside its body the two elements are combined into enough water to keep the animal alive and healthy.

Except for the dozen or so species of kangaroo rat, there seems to be only one other creature that can survive in the desert on a dry diet and without drinking any water at all. This is the small beetle called the powder-post beetle. It lives on dead wood, usually by eating its way into an old tree trunk or a fence post. Tiny heaps of powder below a row of holes in a fallen fence post show that the powder-post beetle has been taking its meals there. Like the kangaroo rat, it manufactures inside its body all the water it needs in order to stay alive.

If you should take an afternoon walk through the desert, you probably would see neither a powder-post beetle nor a kangaroo rat. The beetle is not easy to notice, and the kangaroo rat hides in its burrow all day, out of sight of its enemies, and comes out only at night for its seed-hunting expeditions. But scientists go to a great deal of trouble to find both these creatures so that they can study them in their laboratories. They are especially interested in the kangaroo rat because this "mouse that never drinks" has solved so successfully the problem of living in the dry desert.

People and Deserts

3

People are not so well-equipped for living in the desert as certain plants and animals. People must have water regularly, and more frequently than many plants and animals need it. But people can't manufacture water inside their bodies, and their bodies have no special water-storage compartments.

Of course people can economize on water, and all desert dwellers learn to be good water economizers. They don't use water extravagantly in their everyday life, as people do in other parts of the world. Often, for example, desert dwellers "wash" their dishes with sand instead of water. Sometimes they use sand for "washing" themselves too.

Desert dwellers also know all sorts of tricks for preserving body moisture, the water that is an important

Camel drivers must protect themselves against the baking sun.

part of every cell of the human body. At the United States Army Yuma Test Station, in our American desert country, doctors found that if a man walks for two hours during the heat of a desert day, he sweats out about three quarts of water. To keep from losing water that rapidly, most people living in the desert try to rest in the shade during the hottest part of each day.

Most desert dwellers also protect their bodies from the direct rays of the sun. The men who drive camel caravans across the Sahara, for example, keep themselves completely covered by long cloaks and headcloths. The Bushmen of the Kalahari Desert in Africa smear them-

selves with oil and let the oil become caked with dust so that it forms a protective coating.

But even a man who shields himself from the sun all day, and does not move at all, can't stay alive very long in a desert if he doesn't have fresh water. If the daytime temperature of the desert rises to 100 degrees or more—which often happens—and he has no water to drink, he will probably die in five days or less. If the temperature is not quite so high, he may live a little longer without water, but probably not more than a week.

In other words, all human desert dwellers must have some dependable method for obtaining water regularly in order to keep alive. They may be able to collect water during a rainfall, but desert rainfalls are not dependable. A desert may be without rain for months, even years, at a time. That's why most people who live in a desert use one of the two other methods for obtaining water there. They find water under the desert floor, or they bring it in from outside the desert. Both methods have been used by desert dwellers for many centuries.

Water under the desert floor rises to the surface by itself, at certain places. Sometimes it rises as a bubbling spring. Sometimes it seeps slowly upward to form a shallow water hole. These places of moist soil and flourishing life are called oases, and they look like green islands in a desert sea. Each oasis is surrounded by desert, but it is not really a part of the desert because it is not dry. And people who live in an oasis do not really deserve the name of desert dwellers because they usually have plenty of water.

Most of the people we think of as living in the Sahara, for example, really live in the oases scattered here and there through that vast territory. Some Sahara oases are small, with water enough for only a few families. Some are much larger. An oasis formed by many springs may be so large that several villages can exist inside its green and shady boundaries.

But in desert areas where there are no oases, people can sometimes get water from under the desert floor. Sometimes they find it not very far below the surface.

In Africa's Kalahari Desert the Bushmen look for a low spot in the ground and thrust a hollow reed down into the earth there. If they have chosen the spot well (and they are very skillful at this), they can suck water up through the reed. Sometimes they suck up more than they need to drink. Then they transfer some of it to an empty ostrich shell, which they use as a canteen. After a rain, when the earth is soaked with water, many ostrich shells may be filled and hidden away. Thus the Bushmen will have a supply of water on hand for a long period of drought when the ground dries up entirely.

Some of the cliff-dwelling Indians who lived in the American deserts long ago used another method of obtaining underground water. They dug big wells deep into the desert soil, and cut steps in the walls of the wells so that they could climb down to the bottom and fill their water jars. If a well went dry, they dug it deeper until they struck water again. In a period when no rain fell for a long time, they had to deepen their wells over and over again.

The nomadic tribes that wander from place to place in the Gobi also learned long ago to dig wells. As they traveled about they moved from one well to another.

The second method of obtaining water in the desert, bringing it in from the outside, was used by certain American Indians too.

The Hohokam Indians, who lived in Arizona more than 500 years ago, dug canals to bring water to their desert villages from the nearest river. One canal, supplying a large settlement with water from the Gila River, was thirty feet wide at the top. Its slanting walls went down to a depth of seven feet. Other smaller canals led off from this big one. The Hohokam were so skillful at obtaining water by this method that they have been called the Canal Builders.

Ancient desert dwellers in Iran used this same system, but instead of digging open canals they dug underground tunnels, so that the water would not be evaporated as it flowed along. Some of their tunnels ran for several miles from a spring or some other natural water source. The men who dug those tunnels and kept them in repair more than 2,000 years ago had to burrow through the earth like moles. It was hard and dangerous work. Often they lost their lives when a tunnel collapsed upon them far underground.

Some of those tunnels, called *qanat*, are still being used. Not all ancient systems for obtaining water in the desert have proved so long-lasting. Indian wells in our American deserts sometimes ran dry, no matter how deep they were. The Hohokam canals became worthless if the river which fed them dried up. And although some desert springs have poured forth gallons of water every day for centuries, others have dwindled to tiny trickles or disappeared completely.

That's why the ruins of abandoned towns and villages can be seen today in almost every desert of the world. Men had to leave those places because they could no longer get water there.

But there are many new cities in our deserts today too. Some of them prove that by modern methods men can now obtain water in places once too dry to support life in any form.

Today, with powerful machinery, men can dig wells deeper than ever before. Pipe lines also bring water into our deserts today, sometimes over a distance of hundreds of miles. And today we have huge irrigation systems, usually controlled by the government, that supply water to thousands of desert dwellers.

Those irrigation systems depend on big dams built across deep canyons high in the mountains. Rivers, rain and melting snow, pouring into those canyons, form lakes behind the dams. Then a network of machine-dug canals and ditches carries the lake water to the desert areas at the foot of the hills. Men known as "ditch bosses" measure out the exact amount of water allowed to each property owner.

These vast new irrigation systems make it possible for more people to live in desert regions than could ever live there before. But they only prove, once more, what man learned long ago in ancient times: people can live in deserts only where they can obtain the regular supply of good water that is necessary for human survival.

4

Why Are Deserts Dry?

There are three chief reasons why deserts are dry, and there is a clue that leads us to each of those reasons.

A map of the world is the first clue.

The map shows us that the world's deserts are not just dotted here and there over the earth's surface, in a hit-or-miss pattern. Instead they lie in two broad belts that circle the globe on either side of the equator, one in the Northern Hemisphere and one in the Southern.

Each band begins roughly 2,000 miles away from the equator. Both are close enough to it to have long days of sunshine and warm temperatures. This kind of climate causes water to evaporate quickly.

Therefore, when water does reach the deserts in the form of rain, a great deal of it is lost quickly by evaporation.

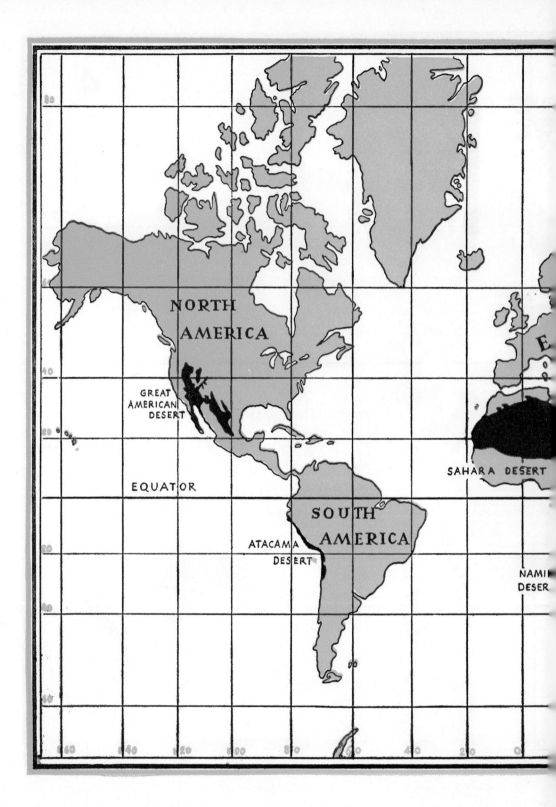

NORTH AMERICA

GREAT AMERICAN DESERT

EQUATOR

SOUTH AMERICA

ATACAMA DESERT

SAHARA DESERT

NAMIB DESER

E

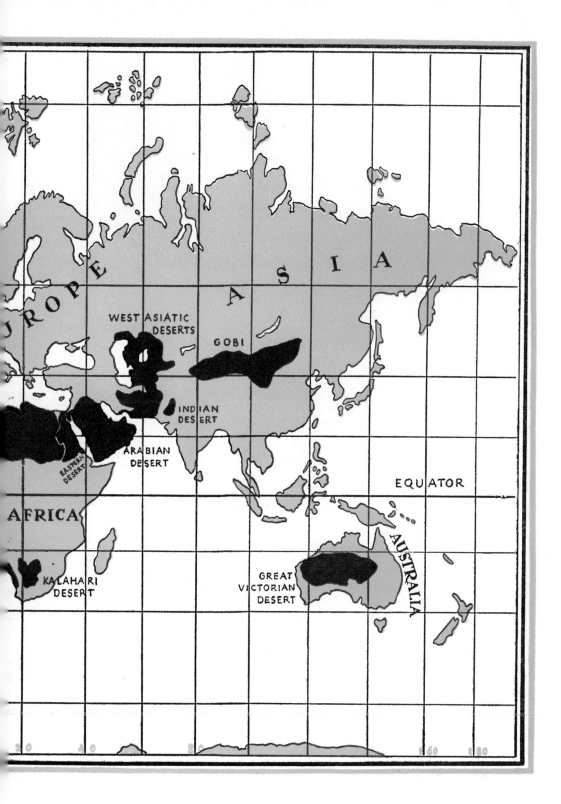

That's why the location of the world's deserts, in those two warm sunny belts, is one reason for their dryness.

But deserts don't get as much rainfall as other parts of the world. There are two chief reasons for this. The clue to the first is the curious name which seafaring men gave to those earth-circling belts many years ago. The sailors called them the "horse latitudes."

Horses were often carried on shipboard in those days for the use of soldiers on their way to battle or colonists on their way to new lands. The horses were likely to die if the ships lay becalmed for many days on a hot still sea, and this often happened in the seas of those two belts. The reason why it happened is that the wind frequently dies down there for days at a time. So the sailors may have given the name "horse latitudes" to those areas because so many horses died there.

Or perhaps the sailors chose the name because any wind that did blow across the seas of those two belts was likely to be rough and changeable. It would veer first in one direction and then in another like a wild horse.

Today nobody knows for sure how the name "horse latitudes" came to be used for those two belts around the globe. But the name helps us remember that there are often no winds in those latitudes, and that the winds that do blow there are likely to be changeable.

These two facts have an important effect on rainfall in the deserts.

Moisture-laden clouds, usually formed above the sea, are the source of the rain that falls on the earth. Those clouds are carried about by the winds. And winds of the horse latitudes sometimes die into a calm, sometimes swirl wildly about. They don't bring rain clouds regularly over all the lands in those latitudes. The areas that get the least rain are our deserts.

Of course the map of the world also shows us that not all the land in the horse latitudes is desert country. Where the northern belt of horse latitudes crosses the United States, for example, there are deserts in Arizona, New Mexico, Utah, Nevada, California and Texas. But east of these states, in the same belt, there are no deserts at all. This is because the winds in the Gulf of Mexico blow more steadily than most horse latitude winds. They blow northward over the Gulf and beyond it, carrying rain clouds with them. Those clouds provide rain for the whole broad Mississippi Valley. Occasionally, mostly during the late summer and fall, those clouds drift as far west as the desert states. When that happens, the deserts of the American Southwest have their brief rainy season. They may have another, even slighter, rainy season in the late winter and early spring.

Our last clue points to the reason why our Southwest almost never gets any rain from moisture-laden clouds blown inland from the Pacific Ocean. This clue can be found on a map showing the geography of that part of the United States. The clue is the chain of mountains that runs like a wall for a thousand miles along the Pacific coast, not far from the shore.

When ocean-born clouds are blown against these mountains and carried up the slopes into the chill air of the high altitudes, they usually lose all their moisture. It forms quickly into raindrops, just as the moisture in the air of a warm steamy room forms quickly into drops of water when it comes in contact with a chilled glass or a cold windowpane. Therefore, the high cold western slopes of those coastal mountains receive a fair amount of rainfall.

But the wind that has blown the clouds inland has become a dry wind by the time it crosses the mountains and reaches the land beyond. It has lost its rain on the western slopes of the mountains and can seldom bring

Western winds lose their moisture as they cross the mountains.

any to the eastern slopes and the land at their feet—the land of our American deserts.

In many parts of the world, mountains stand between a desert and a sea. Those mountains help keep the desert

In some deserts wind and rain have made strange rock shapes.

dry by preventing rain clouds from being blown over. Scientists have a special phrase to describe what those mountains do. They say the mountains "cast a rain shadow" on the lands beyond them—a "shadow" where little or no rain falls.

Every desert is a kind of living record of its own history. The salt and other minerals found in certain deserts, for example, tell us that at some ancient time those areas were not deserts at all, but the floors of lakes or seas. Strange rock shapes standing in other deserts tell us about the centuries of changing weather that wore those rocks into their present weird forms.

One of the most striking chapters in the history of

certain deserts can be read in the piles of crumbled rock and other debris lying at the foot of mountains or volcanoes rising out of an otherwise flat desert floor. In some places this debris, washed down the slopes, has spread out in a layer several thousand feet thick. And this "new" layer over the old desert floor, built up over thousands of years, is growing thicker all the time.

The history of the world's deserts is still being written. All of them are still changing, all the time. The landscape of some deserts changes constantly, for example, because powerful winds pick up clouds of dust and sand at one place and set them down somewhere else.

But no matter how much the deserts change in appearance, they never seem to become less dry. In fact, many scientists think that at least some of the world's deserts, and perhaps all of them, are growing drier all the time.

5

How Dry Is a Desert?

Some deserts are drier than others, mostly because they get less rainfall.

Some deserts, the least dry of them, get as much as ten inches of rainfall a year, or more. Even ten inches of rainfall isn't very much, of course. It is less than one-third the amount of rain that falls annually in most of Iowa and Illinois and Michigan. It is less than one-quarter of the rain that Portland, Oregon, gets, or Little Rock, Arkansas. It is only one-sixth as much rain as falls on most of Alabama and Louisiana.

Some deserts get far less than ten inches of rain a year. Some get less than five inches. There are deserts in the world where it hasn't rained at all for more than ten years at a time.

One interesting thing about the rain that does fall on

deserts is that it is usually followed immediately by bright sunshine and often by a brilliant rainbow. If the rain doesn't last long and if the sunshine that follows is very hot, a desert may lose almost every bit of a rainfall by rapid evaporation.

But even when a rain lasts longer, when a great deal of water falls during a real cloudburst, the desert doesn't hold very much of this precious moisture. A desert doesn't remain damp for days and scattered with huge puddles as other parts of the world often do after a heavy rain. If deserts don't lose by evaporation all the water they receive, they may lose it in two other ways. This depends on whether the water stays on the surface of the ground or sinks into it.

Where the floor of a desert is hard-packed and baked solid by the sun, the water slides over the surface just as water slides over a concrete road. It runs down slopes and along little gulleys, carving the gulleys deeper as it flows.

If several of these rivulets come together, the water in them may form a heavy stream. In our American deserts the channels followed by these streams are called washes or arroyos. The Arabian word for them, used in the Sahara, is *wadi*.

Mesquite bushes grow along the dry, rock-strewn arroyo.

For most of the year an arroyo looks like a deep rock-strewn gash in the desert floor. It may be noticed at all only because there are mesquite bushes growing along it. This thorny desert shrub is usually a sign of damper-than-usual ground. In the spring, when the mesquite puts out its green leaves and greenish-yellow flowers, it makes an arroyo look cool and pleasant.

But a wash can be a very dangerous place. It may be dry as dust for months, and then in just a few minutes it may be filled with a flood of roaring water.

Strangers in desert country are sometimes caught in one of these sudden floods. Often they have no warning that a wall of water is rushing down on them because there has been no rain at all where they are. Desert storms frequently cover only a very small area. This lack of warning is why people have been drowned in flooded arroyos. Some experts think more people have been drowned in this way, in the world's deserts, than have ever died there from thirst.

The water in an arroyo may flow eventually into a river bed. This may be nearly dry or entirely dry except during the brief period when flooded arroyos suddenly give it life.

Or the water in an arroyo may flow into a hollow where it forms a small lake, which will soon dry up from evaporation. Then, in the hot sun, the bed of the temporary lake will split and crack until its surface is covered with elaborate patterns. Such a dried lake bed, very common in some deserts, is called a *playa*.

Sometimes the water in an arroyo disappears because

Soon the same arroyo may be filled with rushing water.

it reaches an area of loose soil, where it sinks into the ground. That particular spot in the desert will be called a sink, and it is usually greener than the rest of the desert because it gets the most water.

Sometimes the stream in an arroyo just flows along, gradually shrinking after the rain stops, until the last bit of it evaporates into the hot dry air.

Where a desert floor is covered over with a layer of loose sand or crumbled rock, rain sinks in very rapidly. The water drops down among the loose particles much more rapidly than rain usually soaks into the rich soil of good farm land. In some deserts it may continue downward until it reaches a layer of hard limestone. There it collects in an underground pool or joins an underground stream.

Under every desert in the world there is water somewhere. But it may be hundreds or even thousands of feet below the surface.

6

Explorers of the Deserts

The men who became famous for exploring the deserts of the world usually set out on their hazardous journeys for one or more of four reasons:

To seek the gold, silver, jewels or other treasures they believed were hidden beneath the desert floor or were held in secret places of the desert.

To chart a travel route so that trade might be carried on between two areas separated from each other by a desert.

To seek information that would add to man's knowledge of the world of today and yesterday.

To answer the challenge the desert made to them, to prove that they could do what no other man had ever done before.

Whatever the reason for their journey, those explorers succeeded only if they had great courage, great endurance, and, in most cases, great good luck. The deserts of the world have destroyed or swallowed up explorers who lacked those qualities. That's why certain sections of the world's deserts are still more or less unknown, except perhaps to native people who long ago learned to survive under the special difficulties of desert life.

In the early 1500s, a Franciscan priest, Marcos de Niza, set off into unknown country to seek the treasure he believed was hidden there.

De Niza was in the service of Antonio de Mendoza, ruler of the new Spanish colony of Mexico. Not long before, Spanish soldiers had conquered Mexico. Already they had sent home to their king great quantities of gold and silver seized from the country's Indian inhabitants. But Mendoza was determined to obtain still more wealth for Spain. Eagerly he listened to rumors about certain cities far to the north. These cities, called the Seven Cities of Cibola, were said to be so rich that their walls were covered with gold and turquoise.

"Find the Seven Cities of Cibola," said Mendoza.

In the year 1539 the priest started forth on his quest, with a few Indian guides and a Negro slave.

Soon after leaving the Spanish settlement at Culiacán, on the west coat of Mexico, the little party came to a waste land of dry stream beds and barren mountains, stretching as far as the eye could see. De Niza didn't know whether human beings could survive a trip across that desert, but he pushed forward. Water was scarce. Food for the pack animals was hard to find. There was little shelter from the blazing sun.

At last, at the end of a journey of hundreds of miles, de Niza stood on a high mesa near the present city of Gallup, New Mexico. In the distance he could see a place said to be called Hawikúh. It was one of the Seven Cities of Cibola. He could see no gold or turquoise on its walls, but he felt sure the city must be very rich because it was so large.

Estevan, the slave, had gone ahead into Hawikúh and had been killed by Zuni Indians. De Niza knew he would suffer the same fate if he tried to enter the city. So he turned about and once more made the long journey back through the desert to Mexico.

The next year a force of Spanish soldiers, led by Francisco de Coronado and with de Niza serving as their guide, conquered the Seven Cities of Cibola. They found them empty of treasure. The scouting parties

Coronado sent out into the surrounding country, in search of other hoards of wealth described in Indian legends, also returned empty-handed.

But those scouting parties were blazing trails across certain desert areas of Arizona and New Mexico never before known to white men. And de Niza and his brave little band are still famous among the great desert explorers of history. De Niza is believed to be the first white man to see part of the great barren waste land that is now called the Sonoran Desert.

Another famous trip of exploration, which started out very near the Seven Cities of Cibola, took place about 300 years after de Niza's historic journey. The purpose of this exploration was to establish a trade route —a wagon and stagecoach road—from the Arizona settlement called Fort Defiance to the Colorado River and the new state of California beyond it. The leader of the expedition was a young naval officer who had fought in the war with Mexico. It was through this war that the United States won much of the territory once claimed by Spain, including the land of our deserts of the Southwest. The officer's name was Edward Fitzgerald Beale.

By the time Beale set out, Spaniards and Americans had been exploring the desert country of Arizona for many years. Parts of it were quite well known. Beale's trip is famous because it was made with camels, the first camels ever introduced into an American desert since prehistoric times when camels ran wild there.

Beale himself suggested using camels for the journey. At first people laughed at this suggestion, but finally the Secretary of War heard about it and decided it was an excellent idea. The Secretary sent men to Egypt, Tunisia and Turkey to buy camels and hire Arab camel drivers, and bring them to the United States.

The animals arrived in fine condition. The drivers, however, were so frightened to find themselves in a strange country that all but one of them returned home immediately.

In the year 1857 Beale and the rest of the trail-blazing explorers left Fort Defiance with the camels and with some horses and mules. For hundreds of miles the party struggled through hot desert and rugged mountains. The route they mapped out was later followed by the builders of the Santa Fe railway line. Later still it was the route for U. S. Highway 66 across Arizona.

All About the Desert

In the spring of 1922, Roy Chapman Andrews, a famous American scientist, set out into the Gobi. He hoped to learn more about the Gobi, one of the least-known deserts in the world, and to map some of its uncharted areas. He also hoped to learn more about prehistoric times on our earth, by finding fossils of dinosaurs that had lived in the Gobi two hundred million years ago.

The American Museum of Natural History in New York helped Andrews organize his expedition. The party consisted of forty men with eight automobiles and with 150 camels to carry supplies and gasoline.

The expedition started into the desert from the small Chinese city of Kalgan, now called Wanchuan. The cars went first. Andrews wanted them to move ahead quickly and establish a camp in the desert as soon as possible. He knew that his expedition would be able to remain in the desert only during the summer. Bitter cold and fierce snowstorms would force his party to leave when winter approached. Behind the cars came the camels carrying extra gasoline and supplies.

Riding in the cars, over hard bumpy desert land, Dr. Andrews and his party pushed steadily northwest. They traveled along an ancient caravan route that connected Wanchuan to Ulan Bator, the capital of Mongolia. Near the middle of the desert, they swung west, leaving the caravan trail to enter a completely trackless and unknown region.

The expedition ran out of water at times. Its gasoline almost gave out. Often the men had to huddle inside their tents, wrapped in blankets, to protect themselves from violent dust storms. They shivered with cold at night, and their skins turned black under the hot daytime sun.

Automobiles and camels were used to explore the vast Gobi.

All About the Desert

As he traveled, Andrews made maps of the uncharted areas he was seeing and took notes describing this unknown land.

And he did find dinosaur fossils. In fact, he proved that the Gobi is one of the best fossil-hunting areas in the world, and one of the best of all sources of information about the past history of our earth. Some of the fossilized dinosaur bones he dug up were different from those discovered in other areas. He also brought back with him the first dinosaur eggs man had ever seen.

Those dinosaur eggs may be seen today in an exciting dinosaur exhibit at the Museum of Natural History in New York. They, and the maps and notes Andrews made, proved the great value of scientific exploration in the desert.

To René Caillié the Sahara Desert was a challenge. More than anything else he wanted to explore its vastness. Caillié was born in France in 1799.

When he was a small boy he saw a map of Africa on which the big areas of the Sahara were marked simply *Desert* or *Unknown*. "Cross me if you dare," the Sahara seemed to be saying to him.

Caillié made up his mind to accept that challenge.

He decided that one day he would travel to Timbuktu. This was a legendary city about which many stories had been told. Actually the people in Europe knew almost nothing about the mythical spot. They believed it was near the southern edge of the Sahara, in the very heart of Africa. René Caillié wanted to go there someday. Then he could come home and tell people he had seen Timbuktu—he, little René Caillié. Then everyone would know that he had done what no European had ever done before.

Caillié was the orphan son of a poor French baker, and his uncle put him to work at an early age to learn bootmaking. The boy's chances of reaching Africa seemed very small. The books he read about the Sahara were also discouraging. In them he learned about the Moslems who lived there and whose camel caravans crossed the desert with cargoes of slaves, ivory, gold, salt, rare woods and animal skins. Those Moslems, the books said, hated Christians so much that they killed them on sight. But Caillié wouldn't give up his dream.

When he was sixteen years old, he worked his way to the West African coast. But the French officials there wouldn't let him go inland. His first two attempts to reach the Sahara ended in dismal failure.

All About the Desert

When he was finally ready for his next attempt on the desert, he made up his mind to travel this time as a Moslem. So to learn the native language, customs and religion, he asked permission to join a nomadic Moslem tribe that wandered about not far from the coast. He didn't dare tell the Moslems that he was a French-born Christian. Instead, he said he was an Egyptian who had been kidnaped as a baby and brought up in France.

Apparently the Moslems believed him. They gave him very little food, beat him constantly, and treated him like a slave. But they let him travel with them. He learned all their ways and could recite Moslem prayers as quickly and correctly as any member of the tribe.

At the end of nine exhausting months, Caillié returned to Senegal and asked French officials there to help him undertake a desert expedition. Now he was sure they would agree that he was well equipped for it. But again they laughed at him and refused his request.

Caillié was now twenty-six years old. Once more his savings were gone, and he seemed no nearer his goal than he had been as a boy of sixteen. But the Sahara still challenged him as it had twenty years earlier. He spent the next year in an indigo factory, earning more money. While working there, he heard that the Paris Geographical Society had offered a prize of 2,000 francs—then about $500—to the first man who could reach Timbuktu and bring back to France accurate information about the city and the routes leading to it.

Caillié wrote in his diary, "Dead or alive the reward will be mine." He decided to reach Timbuktu by a northeasterly route from the west coast of Africa, along the great Niger River. From there he would take a route that led due north across the trackless Sahara to the Mediterranean coast.

Immediately he spent his new hoard of savings to hire native guides and servants and to buy tobacco, beads and other goods for use in trading with the Moslems. Then, fearing that white officials would try to stop him, he made his way to a little coastal settlement where no officials lived. From there, on the morning of April 19, 1827, he set off on his daring journey. A year and a day later Caillié reached Timbuktu.

The city of Timbuktu was a tragic disappointment to him. It was not the beautiful place of jeweled palaces he had dreamed of. It was a dirty town of mud houses and narrow alleys, crowded with 20,000 ragged inhabitants and the caravans that came to and from its sprawling market place.

Timbuktu was a dirty town of mud houses and narrow alleys.

By then Caillié had another disappointment too. He learned that an Englishman, Alexander Gordon Laing, had reached Timbuktu two years earlier. This meant that after all Caillié was not the first European who had laid eyes on the long-sought metropolis of the Sahara.

But Caillié was told Laing had been killed shortly after leaving the city on his way home. So the young Frenchman decided that he could, at least, give Europe its first eyewitness account of Timbuktu. He could if he himself were not killed trying to cross the thousand miles of desert that lay between him and the seacoast.

Caillié sold the last of his goods, hired a guide and bought a camel. As soon as he completed the careful notes he was making on Timbuktu, he set out across the world's greatest desert in the company of his guide and a 600-camel caravan.

From the very beginning he suffered terrible hardships. His treacherous guide stole his water and food and forced him to walk on foot across the blistering desert floor. With cruel glee the man joined with the other Moslems in the caravan when they stoned Caillié for sport and pricked his eyelids with desert thorns.

But day after day, week after week, Caillié struggled on. The sand blinded him. He became so sick with scurvy that he could hardly move. Once he came close to death in a sandstorm. Still he managed somehow to keep up with the caravan, knowing he would surely die if he became separated from it and lost in the desert.

At the end of two months of torture and misery, of desperate thirst and hunger, Caillié reached the hills at the northern edge of the desert. He had crossed the Sahara! Now he was determined to complete his journey.

All About the Desert

Leaving the caravan, and traveling only at night to avoid being murdered as a Christian, Caillié went on alone and finally arrived at Tangier on the Mediterranean coast. He crept into the town four months and three days after leaving Timbuktu, so weak that he could barely drag himself to the door of the French consul's house. But the leather bag clutched in his thin hand held accurate notes on each day of his amazing journey. In them he had described every stretch of sand dunes, every hill, every oasis he had passed during his trip across the Sahara.

Late that same year, 1828, the Geographical Society in Paris honored René Caillié with a great reception. He had won the Society's prize and the respect and admiration of scientists all over the world. He was the first European to reach Timbuktu and return to tell of the adventure. He had succeeded in erasing the word *Unknown* from a part of the world's greatest desert. The small boy who had been challenged by the Sahara had become one of the most famous of all desert explorers.

7

Desert Travel

It is impossible to know who first blazed the most ancient routes of desert travel. Those routes were in existence long before the days of recorded history, centuries before René Caillié and Roy Chapman Andrews followed caravan routes across the Sahara and the Gobi.

But it is easy to guess why the routes were chosen. They were seldom straight lines across the deserts. In each case they moved from oasis to oasis, or from well to well. In other words, each route was developed, perhaps over a long time, by men who were seeking the cross-desert paths that were best supplied with water.

It is also easy to guess that there were no pack-train routes at all across the most arid deserts until man had domesticated the wild camel. That animal is the one best equipped to travel a long distance without water. No one is certain where or when the camel was tamed and trained to carry loads and riders. Probably that happened more than 3,000 years ago in southwestern Asia. And probably the caravan routes of that area are the oldest in the world. Afterward the use of the camel as a pack animal spread throughout Asia and then through North Africa. Soon the deserts there were also crisscrossed by caravan routes.

Not all desert caravans are alike. Some are made up of merchants and traders, others of explorers, still others of pilgrims on their way to some shrine or holy city. In the Sahara, the Iranian and the Arabian deserts, travelers carry their goods on the one-humped camels called dromedaries. In the Gobi they use the two-humped Bactrian camels.

Sahara camels are fed dried dates when there is no forage growing along the way, but Gobi camels receive grain out of a nose bag. Arabian camels sometimes get dried sardines. Sahara camel drivers have a trick of singing to their beasts to urge them along.

But all desert caravans meet the same problems: scarcity of water, dust storms, faintly marked trails sometimes completely hidden beneath drifting sand, illness and death among the animals, and—though less often

In the Gobi, camels receive grain out of a nose bag.

now than in the past—sudden slashing attack by bandits or raiders. Because they do face the same problems, it is possible to learn something about all caravans of today and yesterday by watching just one.

Let's take, for example, a modern caravan leaving the city of Wanchuan in China and crossing the Gobi to Ulan Bator, the capital of Mongolia. This particular caravan is made up of several traders who have joined forces and hired an experienced camel leader, or master, to guide them across the desert.

The camel master is in complete charge of the journey. Like the captain of a ship, his word is law. He selects the route, is responsible for the safety of men and animals and cargo, and owns the pack of fierce dogs that accompany the caravan as guards.

The other men hired for the trip are a chief cook called *Kuo-T'ou*, which means Head of the Pot, a Second Cook, and camel tenders called camel pullers. Each camel puller is in charge of a string of animals called a *lien*. There are seldom more than eighteen animals in a lien because not even the best camel puller can look after more camels than that.

When travelers, cargoes and supplies are all assembled at Wanchuan, the camel pullers load the pack animals. This is a difficult job. Usually two camel pullers work together, loading the beasts in their two strings, one animal at a time. Each camel's load weighs about 350 pounds. First the men divide this load into two equal parts, placing one part on each side of the kneeling animal. Then each camel puller swings half of the load into the sling hanging from his side of the camel's back. Both halves of the load must be slung on the camel at the same time because one half balances the other. When the camel rises, his heavy burden stays on his back because of its perfect balance.

As the caravan leaves Wanchuan, all the camels are in fine condition. Their humps are firm because of the fat stored in them during the period of good grazing since their last journey.

At the head of each string walks its camel puller, tugging at the line attached to a peg in his first animal's nose. All the beasts, those serving as mounts for the traders and those carrying cargo, water and other sup-

Both halves of the load are swung on the camel at once.

plies, plod steadily along in single file, at a swaying gait of about two and one-half miles an hour. The bells on their harness jingle as they move.

At the head of the whole caravan, walks the Head of the Pot, who also takes charge of the guardian dogs. He uses these animals as scouts to alert him to another caravan's approach or to dangers along the way. In very hot country or when bandits are known to be near, the caravan rests during the day and travels only at night with the camels' bells muffled.

When the time has come to eat and rest, the camel master chooses the stopping place. He finds one close to water whenever possible. The Head of the Pot sets up the eating tent and starts the fire on which a meal will be prepared. The Second Cook makes certain that the water supply is drinkable and superintends the re-filling of the big water barrels.

In the meantime, the camel pullers, working in pairs, are unloading their animals so that they too can rest. The men find grazing for the beasts, if any is near by, or feed them with supplies carried for emergencies. If there is no well in the neighborhood, they give the animals a carefully measured ration of water. Then they inspect the camels' feet for blisters or other injuries, and may sew a piece of hide over a sore foot to give it a chance to heal. They watch for pack sores too, and make soft cushion-like bandages to cover them.

When the caravan is ready to move on again, the camels are reloaded, the cooking tent is folded and packed, and the dogs are rounded up. Then the line of march is formed once more, and the caravan continues on its way.

As it travels northward, day after weary day, the camel pullers pass the time by spinning yarn out of the hair their shaggy camels shed continuously, and knitting that yarn into socks. At the end of the long journey, a man may have several pairs of camelhair socks ready to sell in the bazaars of Ulan Bator. The price he receives for them will increase his scant earnings for the trip. And at Ulan Bator the traders in the caravan will sell their goods, too, and buy other products to take back to Wanchuan.

Now a new railroad track connects Wanchuan with Ulan Bator. And in other deserts railroads and roads follow ancient caravan routes.

Desert road-building and track-laying are always an expensive business. This is partly because food and water for the workers can seldom be obtained along the way and must be brought into the desert at high cost. Another reason is the roughness of much desert country, where canyons and rugged hills are often common. A stretch of hard-packed clay or a layer of wind-scoured stones makes road building of all kinds fairly easy. Shifting sand dunes, on the other hand, may make it almost impossible.

It has proved impossible, for example, to build a paved road across the dune regions of the Sahara, called the "moving ground" or *fesh-fesh* areas. At first, road builders tried to bind the sand with tar. But they found the tar melted quickly in the hot desert sun and the sand shifted again under the force of the wind. That's why the trail across that part of the desert is now marked only by desert grass planted along its edges, and by barriers much like the fences used to keep highways clear of snow drifts in other parts of the world. Tall white stone or metal markers, erected every few miles, help to keep the traveler on his way when both grass and fences have been covered over with sand. Alongside these markers is sometimes a grim warning sign that reads *Attention! No water for 100 miles!*

Because of such difficulties and because of the high cost, roads and railroads are seldom built in deserts even today except where they are absolutely necessary. If a rich new mine is opened up in the heart of a desert, a railroad may be built to the mine no matter how costly the job proves to be. Both roads and railroads cross the deserts of America's Southwest, because they are needed for the nation's trade and industry and for the tourists who enjoy exploring our desert areas.

But the Kalahari Desert in Africa has no real roads. Neither has the desert heart of Australia. And in the tremendous Sahara there are fewer roads than there are in the small state of Delaware. The Sahara's roads total only some 3,000 miles, including the two main routes that cross the desert from north to south. But where the roads exist, they permit travelers to accomplish in a single day a journey that would take two or three weeks by camel.

Before setting forth upon those Sahara roads, vehicles are carefully checked at the beginning of the trip. They must carry emergency supplies of water and motor fuel, tools and repair parts, devices for digging wheels out of soft sand, water buckets, and ropes long enough to lower those buckets into deep wells. Without such equipment vehicles are not permitted to start the long dangerous journey.

Camel pullers eat and sleep in the court of the caravansary.

In the Sahara there is also a system for checking cars from point to point by radio. If a car fails to arrive at a certain radio post when it is expected, a rescue vehicle is sent out to look for it. The rescue car may have difficulty too, and in that case a second car will follow it. Airplanes fly over the route, if necessary, to locate a missing party.

Cars used for desert travel are usually equipped with special cooling systems and sometimes with special tires.

One variety of desert tire was made by measuring a camel's big foot and comparing its area to the animal's weight. Then an unusually fat tire was designed so that its area was in that same proportion to the weight of the car.

Caravansaries, or inns for caravan travelers, have existed for hundreds of years in many desert areas. Usually they are built around a big inner court in which camels and dogs can be safely enclosed for the night. Sometimes camel pullers build their own fires in the court, eat there, and sleep on the ground rolled up in their blankets. Their employers may rent one of the small rooms around the court and eat in the inn's restaurant.

In the Sahara today this kind of inn, called a *funduq*, may have electric lights and other conveniences expected by modern travelers. Now luxurious buses park in the court alongside rows of ill-smelling, sleeping camels. The air-conditioned motels in America's deserts of the Southwest are modern versions of the ancient caravansaries. Some of them replace old inns where desert wagon trains stopped on their way to new settlements or gold fields a century or more ago.

Airplane travel, of course, has proved very valuable

in the desert. A desert army post, for example, may receive large quantities of its supplies by air. Visitors now fly in a few hours to many once-remote places, perhaps to see the ruins of an ancient city, perhaps to enjoy the hot dry sunshine of a desert resort like Palm Springs in California. But air transportation, especially for heavy freight, is still too expensive for most desert dwellers to use very often.

Another modern form of desert transportation, quite similar to ancient methods of irrigation, is the pipe line. Now huge metal pipes are used to carry water to certain desert towns and to carry gas and oil across desert areas. In Arabia oil travels almost 1,100 miles through a thirty-inch pipe reaching from the desert oil wells to a Mediterranean port.

But there are still great expanses of the world's deserts which are not crossed by such modern travel routes as roads, railroads, pipe lines, or regular air lanes. Some of these areas are so desolate that they are seldom if ever crossed by human beings. No man has any reason to enter them. Other areas echo occasionally to the noise of a bouncing jeep, which can travel over roadless country that is not too rough or hilly. Still others are crossed today, as they have been for centuries, only by pack trains of animals. The best desert travelers are camels, llamas, or other beasts of burden such as the sturdy burros of Mexico and our own Southwest.

Camels, llamas and burros may some day be crowded off the main travel routes of the world's deserts. But probably there will always be places where desert travel is done with the help of animals or not done at all.

Some deserts are crossed only by pack trains of burros.

8

The Fruit of the Desert

Long before René Caillié made his way to Timbuktu, the Sahara was producing huge crops of the sweet brown dates which men called the most valuable fruit of the desert. The date palm also flourished in the deserts of ancient Arabia, Babylonia and Egypt. It is a tall tree crowned with shining green leaves that rustle in the wind. Today that tree is still the most important source of food and wealth in many desert areas of northern Africa and southwest Asia. It has become an important product in American deserts too.

The date palm's fruits grow on strings, threadlike stems that hang in clusters from the tip of a single stalk. Each cluster is larger than a man's head and contains as many as 1,000 fruits.

Dates can be eaten fresh or dried and kept for a long

Dates grow on threadlike stems that hang in clusters.

time. They are more than half sugar and are so rich in fat and protein that a small handful of them, or a small cake of pressed dates, makes a satisfying meal. Their pits, roasted and ground, can be made into a drink resembling coffee.

But the date palm does a great deal more than produce food. Its leaves may be woven into baskets and mats, or used to thatch a roof. Its stem fibers can be twisted into rope. When the tree dies, its tall trunk, sometimes eighty feet long, makes valuable lumber and firewood. And for as long as the tree lives, it gives welcome shade in lands where shade is rare. Other fruit trees—orange, lemon and lime, for example—are sometimes grown in that shade, and those trees in turn may shade patches of vegetables and flowers at their feet.

Date palms can grow successfully only in a climate that is absolutely dry during summer and fall months. If there is even a slight dampness in the air during the period when the fruit is ripening, the crop may be ruined. But the roots of date palms need a great deal of moisture because the trees are not good water economizers. One palm may send as much as 500 quarts of water a day through its broad green leaves. It will die if it does not get large quantities of water regularly through its roots. The Arabs say that a date palm must have its head in the sun and its feet in the water to grow and bear fruit.

These two needs—dry air and wet soil—are met naturally in only certain desert areas. In the oases of the Sahara, for example, and in similar oases in Asia, the weather is always dry during summer and fall, and a good supply of water exists just underneath the desert floor. That's why date palms flourish in those oases.

The hundreds of thousands of date palms that grow in some large oases are a major source of income for oasis inhabitants. Sixty trees will support one family.

Saharan date groves are so valuable that foreigners often buy them as a sound investment.

In the year 1890 the United States Department of Agriculture imported some date palms into this country and first introduced American farmers to date culture. Fifty years later the desert valleys of California and Arizona were producing twenty million pounds of dates every autumn.

These desert valleys had the very dry summer and autumn climate which a date palm requires, but not all had abundant water close to the surface. The new trees were able to thrive there only because modern machinery and methods could supply the necessary quantities of water. In California's Coachella Valley desert, the big date groves are fed by water from deep machine-drilled wells and from a branch of the machine-dug All American Canal, which carries water 130 miles from the Colorado River.

Modern machinery helps date growers in other ways too. When the fruit is forming, tractors move through the palm groves pulling tall metal towers from tree to tree. Workers standing on those towers cover each cluster of fruit with a paper bag, or cone, to protect it during the ripening period. Later the same tractor-pulled towers lift men into the trees again to harvest the crop.

Large-scale irrigation projects, like those which now help produce America's date crop, also help produce many other crops in once-desert areas—crops such as grapefruit, oranges, cantaloupes, grapes, asparagus, squash, tomatoes, lettuce and cotton. Alfalfa grows so swiftly in the hot sunshine of some irrigated desert areas that it can be cut eight or ten times a year, and give a yield of a ton an acre at every cutting.

The date is still one of the most valuable fruits of the desert. But today the world's newly-irrigated deserts can bring forth fruits of many varieties and in rich abundance.

9

The Desert Cowboy

Men herd cattle in many of the world's deserts, but the best known of all desert cowboys is the one who lives and works in our own American Southwest. The leather chaps he wears and his wide-brimmed hats and high-heeled boots are famous even in distant lands.

The cowboy doesn't dress for show. Like all desert dwellers, he chooses his clothes because they are sensible for desert wear.

His chaps, for example, take their name from the thickets of low bushes and trees, called chaparral, which cover certain desert areas of the American Southwest. The cowboy wears chaps because they protect him as he rides through thorny desert growth. His wide-brimmed hat provides shade from the desert sun. His high-heeled boots make it easier for him to keep his feet in the stirrups as he rides the range all day.

The cowboy's costume is almost as old as the history of cattle raising in the Southwest. That began more than 400 years ago when Spanish missionaries brought the first herds of cows into Arizona. For a time the animals were valuable chiefly for their hides, which were tanned for leather. Today they are valuable chiefly as a source of beef.

Riding herd on desert cattle is a safer job now than it was in the old days when there were few fences and few laws in that part of the country. Then gunfights between cowboys and cattle rustlers sometimes developed into feuds that lasted for years. Nineteen men died in the famous Tewksbury-Graham feud that began, people said, over stolen cattle. Wyatt Earp, who became a United States marshal, was famous for his part in another long feud during those days of the old Wild West.

Today cattle are fenced in, laws are enforced, and marauding cattle thieves appear more often in the movies than in real life. Cowboys no longer have to carry guns to protect themselves. If they carry guns

The cowboy's chaps protect him from the thorny desert brush.

now, it is only for the protection of their herds against bobcats and the mountain lions that sometimes appear in that part of the country.

But desert cattle ranches have not changed very much. They are not like cattle farms in less dry parts of the country, where many cattle can feed in one lush green pasture. In desert country animals have to graze over a wide area, searching for the few desert plants that are good to eat. If a range has already been grazed over for years, so that the naturally sparse desert plants have become sparser than ever, eighty acres of ground may provide food enough for only one animal.

That's why cattle ranches in the Southwest are often very large. And that's why cowboys have to ride many miles a day, to check their herd and to make sure that the tanks which supply it with water are never empty.

A busy highway may run straight across a large desert ranch, but the strangers riding along it will seldom notice any cows along the road and may not even guess that they are passing a ranch. And the cowboy who is tending the herd may not get close to the road for days at a time. In fact he may not see another human being for weeks, unless he happens to meet a shepherd guiding a flock of sheep cross-country from lowland winter grazing grounds to higher summer pastures.

That's why the job of most cowboys today—unless they work on dude ranches and look after guests instead of cattle—is still lonely and rugged and hard. It's no wonder that the American cowboy remains one of the world's favorite heroes.

10

Africa's Deserts

In Africa there are two deserts, one in the north and one in the southwest. The one in the north, the Sahara, is the largest desert in the world.

Imagine a land a thousand miles wide, stretching across the widest part of Africa and you have the Sahara Desert. It reaches from the Atlantic Ocean on the west to Egypt's valley of the Nile on the east. Some geographers prefer to use the name Libyan Desert for the eastern portion, which covers Libya and part of Egypt. But the Libyan Desert is really a part of this one great expanse of sand, gravel and hills. It measures 3,000 miles from end to end and occupies 3,650,000 square miles. That is more than one-quarter of the entire continent.

On the south the Sahara merges gradually into a less dry region called the Sudan. On the north it stops more abruptly at the foot of the green hills rising between the desert and the Mediterranean Sea.

Scientists think that at some time, far in the past, at least part of the land south of those hills was also covered with green grass and green forests. There they have found thousands of ancient rock paintings. These tell the story of people who lived here long ago in what was then a lush, moist country.

But now the desert deserves its Arabic name, Sahara, which means "emptiness" or "nothing." The people of the Sahara live mostly around its edges and in its oases and mountainous areas. The population numbers only about one million. Europe, which is about the same size as the Sahara, has a population of more than 530 million.

Some of the desert's inhabitants are descended from Negro slaves brought into the area from the Sudan. Others are descended from the many people who have, since the dawn of history, conquered the green north coast of Africa and tried to establish power over the vast area below it.

One early group who moved into Africa about 3,000 years ago were the Berbers. They were probably related to the ancestors of southern Europeans. There are still tribes of these sturdy folk, some blue-eyed and light-skinned, others darker, living in and around the Sahara today. Other ancient invaders of North Africa were the seagoing Phoenicians, the Romans, the Byzantines from the east, the Vandals from the North, the Arabs and the Turks. Some of these people left behind only slight signs of their conquest, but the Arabs brought their religion with them and made all of the Sahara a Moslem region. During the past few centuries the Sahara has also been influenced by Spain, Italy, England and France, which took over sections of North Africa and brought new ways of life even into the desert.

The Sahara itself has always had strong defenses against invaders in the form of areas almost impassable to men or beasts or machines. One group of these barriers are the sandy wastes which almost completely cover the northern part of the desert and reach long branching arms down into it. Altogether they make up about one-seventh of the desert. The Arab name for a sandy area is *erg*, and on some maps these regions are named. There is, for example, the Grand Erg Occidental, or Great Western Erg, and the Grand Erg Oriental, or Great Eastern Erg.

In these sandy areas, you will find the Sahara's famous

Sand dunes in the Sahara stretch like waves in a sea.

sand dunes. They are great wavelike hills of wind-blown sand that may measure hundreds of feet from base to crest. In some places these dunes stretch on for many miles, like a great motionless sea of rippled sand.

Here too, in the Grand Erg Oriental, travelers may hear the mysterious and frightening sound known as "singing sands" or "drumming sands." This sound is caused by untold billions of grains of sand sliding down the steep faces of the dunes. The echoes set up by thousands of dune valleys multiply the sound until it becomes a loud pulsating boom.

Often travelers hear strange echoes as the sand shifts.

The Sahara also contains thousands of square miles of another sort of waste land. These are the flat stony plains, like the one called the Tanezrouft, whose vast deadly monotony is not broken by a single shrub or blade of grass. Travelers along the major north-south route that crosses the Tanezrouft have long called this arid waste "The Country of Fear."

On a map of that region only one name appears. It is Bidon 5, which means "Can 5." The word *bidon* is French, and the story behind this name is part of the history of the French occupation of North Africa. It was the French who first experimented with motor transport through this fearsome area during the 1920s. They found the Tanezrouft easier to cross by car than the dune regions. But they had to solve the difficult problem of providing cars with enough fuel to take them across this great expanse. They did this by slowly building up hoards of gasoline cans at stations called Can 1, Can 2 and so forth. Later, as cars improved and needed refueling less often, they abandoned the stations one by one. Now only Bidon 5 remains, right in the center of the empty Tanezrouft.

The Sahara has mountains too. One of its most rugged mountainous regions is the one called Tassili-n-Ajjer. This is a large area of rocky peaks that contains several of the surprises for which this desert is famous. Here, for example, is the canyon of Tamrit, an enormous chasm that plunges 2,000 feet into the earth. Here too, and even more surprising, is an abundance of good soft water—enough of it to form a number of small lakes. Their shores are thick with wild ducks and sheep, and their waters are alive with fish.

The Sahara's greatest mountains lie almost at its center, in an area called the Hoggar at the southern tip of Algeria. The terrible volcanic peaks of the Hoggar show

Peaks of the Hoggar are eroded into weird, frightening shapes.

many weirdly frightening shapes. They rise to almost 10,000 feet and cover a territory 300 miles long and 200 miles wide. The Hoggar seems to tower out of the Sahara like some monstrous, impenetrable fortress. In fact, much of it has never been explored even today, except by men who have peered down at it from planes flying overhead.

In and around that rocky fortress live some of the

All About the Desert

Sahara's strangest inhabitants—the blue-veiled Tuareg. These nomadic tribes are an offshoot of the Berber people. Probably they retreated to the desert centuries ago, rather than accept defeat from one of the numerous foreign forces that invaded the north coast of Africa. They met the modern guns of the French with such ancient weapons as lances, long swords and daggers, and protected themselves only with antelope-hide shields. Nevertheless until very recently they withstood every attempt to subdue them.

The Tuareg still retain their own ways of life, which are different from those of the other Berbers or those of the Arabs. For example, Tuareg women, unlike most Moslem women, do not wear veils. It is the Tuareg men who cover their faces below the eyes with a scarf of the same dark blue color as their long robes. This *litham*, as the scarf is called, may be worn as a protection against the desert dust. But no one really knows why a Tuargi almost never permits his face to be seen, even in the privacy of his own tent.

The Tuareg have always believed that work is dishonorable. They keep slaves, or vassals, to tend the fields and palm trees in their oases and to guard their herds of sheep, goats and camels. They believe that the

Several warlike desert tribes wear heavy veils below the eyes.

only honorable occupation for men is fighting. For centuries they lived by raiding caravans and oases—unless they had been paid to protect them—and by raiding their enemies and each other. Their magnificent riding camels, called *mehara*, were the best trained and swiftest mounts in the desert. On these they dashed out of their strongholds to terrorize travelers and settlements and vanished just as quickly with their captured wealth.

The men of another group of warlike Berbers called the Blue Moors, also wear veils. For years they were a menace to the huge camel caravans carrying salt mined in the great salt pans at Taoudeni, near the Tanezrouft, to Timbuktu on the southern edge of the Sahara.

Those who finally began to subdue both the Tuareg and the Blue Moors were the tough native soldiers organized into a Camel Corps by the French authorities. By now this police force has made most of the Sahara safe for travelers. There are still sections of this vast desert that strangers are warned to avoid, for fear of raiders, and where caravans use armed escorts. But now more tourists each year cross the Sahara in luxurious air-conditioned buses. They know the most serious danger they are likely to meet is the boredom of a long hot wait while their skilled driver changes a tire, or digs his wheels out of a patch of soft drifted sand.

The boundaries of Africa's second desert, the Kalahari Desert in the southwest, are vague. The reason for this is that its edges are not so dry as the central part, and people disagree as to where the true desert begins. Some say it covers 200,000 square miles. Others say it is twice that size.

Lying on a high plateau, crisscrossed by dry river beds and dotted with low hills, the Kalahari has a number of the shallow depressions, called "pans," which give it its name. Kalahari means "salt pans" in a native tongue. These pans collect a little water when the desert's few scant rains fall during its summer season, which starts in October. Then dry bushes turn green and grasses spring up. Herds of wild grazing animals come down into the Kalahari from the greener lands to the north. There are thousands of them—springbok

Herds of wild grazing animals come into the Kalahari Desert.

gazelles, and various African members of the antelope family, including kudus, steenboks, hartebeests, elands and gnus or wildebeests. After them come their meat-eating enemies: lions, leopards, wild dogs and hyenas. When the Kalahari is green, it is one of the best game areas in the world.

But as winter approaches, the water pans dry up and the green growth shrivels. Then the plant-eaters move back north, and the meat-eaters follow. Then again the Kalahari becomes an unusually arid expanse of red sandy soil, blown up into drifting dunes here and there.

The Kalahari's extreme dryness, especially during the winter, is of great interest to scientists because the Kalahari is what they call a "young desert." By this they mean that only a few hundred years ago its dry river beds flowed with life-giving water. Today those beds are dry even during the rainy season, and scientists say this desert is growing drier all the time.

It was already very dry in 1849 when it was first crossed by a European, Dr. David Livingstone. That famous Scottish missionary and explorer had been told that the desert's water holes were sometimes as much as 100 miles apart. That's why he set out in ox-drawn wagons carrying a large supply of water. But the desert proved even drier than he thought. It was so dry that his oxen died of thirst not long after the start of the journey. Dr. Livingstone had to complete his daring trip by walking across much of the desert on foot.

Today about the only white men who venture far into the Kalahari are the British officers in command of a corps of native desert police. These men work for the government of Bechuanaland, a British protectorate which includes most of the Kalahari. Their lives are not easy. They live mostly on the game they shoot. They can cover their vast territory only by riding camelback and using camels as pack animals to carry their water supply. If they approach a group of the primitive desert natives, they may find themselves showered with poisoned arrows. But if they call out a friendly greeting as they draw near, the natives usually make them welcome.

About three million natives live in the Kalahari. Some are farmers. Some are nomads who travel with their herds in search of pasture. Some are very primitive people who own no animals at all except fierce hunting dogs and who live entirely by hunting.

One group of primitive Kalahari hunters, called Bushmen, live almost exactly as their ancestors did thousands of years ago. They are not even organized into tribes. Each family group wanders alone through the desert.

Bushmen wear almost no clothes and build only temporary shelters out of bush branches and grass. The only things they obtain by trade with their more civilized neighbors are knives, bright necklaces and iron cooking pots. Otherwise their only possessions are water canteens made of ostrich eggs, and simple weapons such as spears, throwing clubs, and bows and arrows. They tip their homemade spears and arrows with poison.

The Bushman is a remarkably good finder of water. Even in the dry season he usually seems to know just where to thrust a hollow reed into the ground to bring up at least a few sips of water. And when no water can be found anywhere he can always locate the unmarked spot where he buried, perhaps many months earlier, an emergency supply of water-filled ostrich eggs, or a few juicy wild melons.

The Bushman is also a superb hunter. He will stalk a wild animal patiently for many hours, moving behind a branch held in front of his body as camouflage. When he finally closes in on his quarry, he may send his dogs in to make the kill, or he may use his spear or his bow and arrows. Sometimes a wounded animal runs on for many miles before the poison in the arrow tip takes effect and it falls dead. The Bushman follows doggedly, no matter how far the animal runs, and covers the dead beast with branches when he has tracked it down. Then the hunter returns for his family and brings them all to the spot to join in a feast, around a fire started by twirling a stick against a block of soft wood.

Bushmen of the Kalahari make water canteens of ostrich eggs.

A Bushman can hit a bird on the wing at a distance of 150 feet with his throwing club. He knows how to dig traps, or pitfalls, along animal trails, and insert poison-tipped stakes in the bottom to kill the victims that fall into them. He finds wild honey by catching a bee, gluing a tiny feather to it, and then following the bee until it leads him to its hoard.

When the Bushman finds an ostrich nest, it is a signal for great rejoicing. He hides near the nest until he has killed both male and female birds. Then he and his family make a fine meal out of the flesh of the birds and their huge eggs. Afterward they make bowstrings out of the ostrich sinews, store water in the empty eggshells, and use the feathers as money for trading purposes.

11

The Deserts of Asia

All of Asia's deserts together do not equal the size of the Sahara. Yet Asia has more separate desert areas than any other continent.

Some of its smaller deserts are the Thar, or Indian Desert, a stretch of rolling sand hills in northwest India; the twin deserts of Iran's high central plateau, Dasht-i-Lut and Dasht-i-Kavir; and the twin deserts of the Turkestan lowlands of the Soviet Union, called Kara-Kum and Kyzyl-Kum. (*Dasht*, a Persian word, and *kum*, a Russian word, both mean "desert.") Larger deserts exist in the Arabian Peninsula.

The largest of all Asian deserts is the Gobi. Its name means "the great desert." That's why it is often called simply *Gobi*, and not *Gobi Desert*.

For 1200 miles it sprawls from east to west across

the heart of the continent. It lies partly in the Independent People's Republic of Mongolia and partly in the section of China called Inner Mongolia. Part of the Gobi is more than a mile above sea level, on a vast plateau where the temperature falls below zero in winter. All of it is swept by ferocious winds that pile up huge sand dunes here and there. Some of those dunes now cover up whole cities of an ancient desert civilization.

The western reaches of the Gobi, the area sometimes called the Taklamakan Desert, have enough water to support plant life. There, and in some of the central parts too, the desert floor is sparsely covered with a tough variety of grass, thorn bushes and other shrubs. The eastern part of the Gobi is more desolate. Water is found there only at a few wells and marshy places. Much of it tastes so salty and bitter that people drink it only if they are desperate with thirst.

Part of the desert's southern boundary is the Great Wall of China. This amazing stone wall, 1900 miles long, was constructed by the Chinese twenty centuries ago. For many hundreds of years it protected them from their Mongol enemies to the north. Then, early in the thirteenth century, hordes of Mongols on tough shaggy horses thundered down over the desert. Led by the great warrior, Genghis Khan, they swarmed over the wall.

Today the Great Wall is no longer important as a military defense, but it is still one of the most remarkable structures in the world. The roadway running along its 15-foot wide top is still used in many places.

The sturdy Mongol nomads, who live in and around the Gobi, are as good horsemen today as their ancient conquering ancestors. Their horses are their proudest possessions; horse racing is their favorite sport; and they consider horse stealing the worst of all crimes. But they also own sheep, and some tribes own oxen and camels too.

Today some of those herdsmen sell wool and hides to the factories being opened up in Ulan Bator. Now, when they visit that ancient caravan center, they see a new railroad station, new industries, electric lights and other signs of modern life. If the present search for large quantities of oil and minerals under the Gobi is successful, the Mongols may even see modern industrial methods introduced right in the heart of the desert. Already the Mongolian government is urging them to join big cattle-raising programs, to send their children to school and to settle down in permanent homes.

But not many of these rugged nomads have as yet abandoned their old ways of life. They like the freedom of open spaces, and most of them still wander around from place to place, just as their ancestors did, on a constant search for pasture for their animals.

When they find a good pasture they hastily build a snug circular shelter, called an *aul* or *yurt*, made of felt or fur stretched over a light framework woven of wood. Rugs are spread over its dirt floor, and wealthy Mongols decorate their walls with embroidered tapestries.

Most Mongol nomads are Buddhists, and there is often a statue of Buddha at the aul's entrance, with a prayer wheel beside it. (A prayer wheel is a cylinder mounted on a wooden handle in such a way that the cylinder can turn.) On it is carved or painted the prayer, *Om! ma-ni pad-me hu-ng*, which means "Hail! jewel in the lotus flower." Mongol Buddhists believe that it is important to speak or see this prayer as often as possible. That's why they often carry small prayer wheels in their hands, spinning them as they walk. And that's why they turn their larger prayer wheels

In the Gobi, Mongols live in circular shelters called yurts.

each time they pass them at the door of a house or a
temple.

A Mongol nomad wears a warm long-sleeved coat,
belted at the waist, over a shirt and wool-lined trousers
tucked into high boots. As the weather grows colder,
he adds extra layers of clothing under the coat. His
boots, loose at the top, serve as pockets for his small

personal possessions—spoons, pipes and tobacco, even a drinking bowl. Mongol women dress like the men, except that they don't wear a belt. The Mongol word for woman means "beltless one."

The more primitive Mongol tribes believe in bathing only twice in a lifetime, once at birth and once before marriage. Because of this dislike of bathing, their naturally reddish-yellow skins turn darker as they grow older.

The Mongols' favorite drink is tea, which they import from China in bricks of tightly pressed dried leaves. With the tea they mix *ghi*, which is boiled and often rancid butter.

Except for tea, these nomads live chiefly on the food obtained from their animals—milk, cheese and mutton. They eat only when they are hungry, rather than at regular meal times, but they can eat a great deal. Three or four hungry men may consume a whole roasted sheep.

Mongol nomads leave their auls open, if they go away for a time, with a supply of food placed just inside the door for passing strangers. The rugged land where they live has taught them to be tough and sturdy themselves, and to share generously with all others who must endure the Gobi's fierce winds, its hot summer sun and its winter cold.

When people speak of the Arabian desert, they usually mean several large arid areas that cover most of the Arabian Peninsula and overlap into the neighboring countries of Jordan, Iraq and Syria. The total desert area on the Arabian Peninsula is about 500,000 square miles. Most of it, divided into three deserts, is found in the country of Saudi Arabia.

Two of these deserts, the Syrian and the Nafud, are in the northern part of that country. The third, the desert of Rub al Khali, or Great Sandy Desert, occupies the southern end of the peninsula. This is the region known as the "empty quarter." It is 250,000 square miles of hot desolation crossed only by small nomadic tribes who alone know the position of the few wells and the trails leading to them.

Arabia's two northern deserts are separated from the great Rub al Khali by a broad belt of hilly land running across the peninsula from east to west. Here are the Tuwaiq Mountains, which catch most of the scant rainfall that the whole peninsula receives. The water which seeps into the ground at the foot of those mountains then flows out into the desert. There it rises to the surface in springs or wells and creates oases. At some wells the water is raised by modern pumps to irrigate grain fields and date palm groves. At others camels and donkeys still plod around and around, day and night, operating primitive water wheels.

In this hilly country, and in the oases at its feet, are the Arabian Peninsula's most important cities and two-thirds of its population. Today some of these Arabs work in gold mines so old that they may have furnished wealth for King Solomon. Others operate modern lathes, pumping stations and generating plants. The great oil industry that has sprung up here, on the east coast, has created new ways of life for these people whose history goes back many thousands of years.

Today, from the booming oil port of Damman on the Persian Gulf, the Arabian Peninsula's only motor road and only railroad run through that band of hills. The single-track railroad crosses less than half of the peninsula, to end at the Arabian capital, Riyadh. The road reaches the opposite shore, at the port of Jidda on the Red Sea.

Along that road, still largely unpaved, lies the great

Hofuf oasis, which has some fifty bubbling springs and 100,000 inhabitants, and the holy city of Mecca to which all Moslems hope to make a pilgrimage before they die. Once all pilgrims had to reach Mecca by camel caravans, some of which stretched out for miles across the sands. Now most pilgrims travel from Jidda to Mecca by this motor road, along which young Arabs drive trucks and buses as skillfully as their fathers guided camels.

Outside this band of hills, live tribes of Arabian nomads, called Bedouin. They scorn the safer, easier lives of the oasis and city dwellers and continue the ancient ways of their ancestors.

Every Bedouin tribe, headed by a leader called a *sheik*, lays claim to its own special section, or *dirah*, of the desert. Each dirah is about 125 miles wide and 200 miles long, and contains at least a few wells or springs. From June to October, when the thermometer climbs to about 120 degrees almost every day, the tribe remains close to its water supply. Then, when the rains come, it packs up its tents and leads its herds out to pasture on the quick green growth spread briefly over the barren desert floor.

A Bedouin's tent, woven of goat hair or sheep wool,

dyed black or brown, can be set up swiftly and just as swiftly taken down. It is supported by stakes driven into the ground and braced by ropes. The sides can be lifted to admit desert breezes or lowered to keep out the bitter cold of a desert night. Curtains form the walls of its separate sections, one for the men, another for the women and children.

The Bedouin's herds are his greatest wealth. He seldom owns one of the famous Arabian horses because they are very expensive. A single horse costs as much as ten good pack camels. And, besides, horses are not well suited to desert life. They can't go very long without water. They can't graze on the harsh desert growth. And their hoofed feet sink too deeply into the sand.

The Bedouin's animals are camels, goats and sheep. Like the nomad in the Gobi and the Sahara, he depends on the camel as his beast of burden, spins camel's hair into thread and rope, and uses camel dung as fuel for his campfires.

His sheep supply him with wool, and his goats provide the milk and cheese which are important parts of his diet. He almost never kills an animal in order to eat its meat. But if a camel, for example, is killed

A Bedouin's tent is woven of goat hair or sheep wool.

accidentally or is slaughtered because he is too old to work, the Bedouin feasts on its tough meat, saves the fat in the hump for cooking, and uses the hide for water bags, belts and sandals.

The other chief items in an Arab's diet, besides milk and cheese, are dates and a thick paste made by boiling maize, millet or sorghum flour in salted water. Many Bedouin tribes own their own date groves. Others must trade wool or some other valuable item for this vital food of the desert. Those living near the coast eat dried or salted fish occasionally, and all Bedouin kill and eat whatever scarce wild game they can find, such as gazelles, wolves, foxes, weasels, hyenas and desert lizards. When a locust plague descends on the desert, they gather as many of these insects as possible. One of their favorite foods is dried locusts.

Arab nomads are suspicious of most visitors to their camps, but if an honored and trusted guest arrives, he is served strong spiced Arabian coffee, brewed in a long-spouted pot over a small fire in the sand. In the meantime the women are preparing the finest feast the tribe can afford.

When a wealthy sheik is entertaining an important guest, he may even order one of his animals to be killed and roasted. One very elaborate Arabian feast, which needs many hours of preparation, consists of a roast camel stuffed with a sheep, which has been stuffed with a fowl, which has been stuffed with eggs.

The food is served on huge platters set on the carpeted sand floor of the men's side of the sheik's tent. The host, his guests and the older men of the tribe sit on pillows around them and scoop the food up with the bare fingers of the right hand. When they have eaten their fill, the younger men of the tribe take their places. The remains of the feast are finally removed to another part of the tent to be finished by the women and children.

Until fairly recently almost all Bedouin tribes were

fierce raiders. They raided each other and raided the wealth-laden caravans crossing the desert. Today strong government forces, equipped with armored cars and planes, have put a stop to much of the raiding. Even today, however, a daring sheik, driven by his love of fighting or the poverty of his tribe, sometimes attempts a swift attack on a rich oasis. He knows that he and his people will be punished by law if they are caught with stolen animals or other booty. But he also knows that he has a fair chance of escaping into the vast trackless regions which are known only to skillful riders of sturdy desert camels.

12

The Deserts of Australia

Dry, flat, hot desert covers most of the heart of Australia inside the green ring of mountains that rises almost all the way around the continent's coast. Part of it is sandy and part stony. Low stone-capped hills divide this desert into several sections that have their own names on a map. In the southwest is the Great Victorian Desert. In the northwest is the Great Sandy Desert. Near the center of this huge island are the Gibson, Arunta, and Simpson deserts. But the few people who have traveled through those waste lands agree that it is usually hard to tell one from the other.

Australia's rainy season lasts from April to October. During that period rivers flow into some of these deserts from the coastal hills, and shallow salty lakes form here and there. But the river beds are usually dry. The lakes are often no more than salty marshes. Eucalyptus or gum trees grow along the rivers, and every breeze stirs the loose strips of bark that hang from their trunks and branches. Stiff spikey grasses and leathery-leaved plants form a dense scrub over huge areas which Australians call "the bush." This is the home of snakes and lizards, and of grass-eating kangaroos and their smaller relatives, the wallabies.

Today Australia's central deserts are empty places. Railroad, highway and airplane routes go around them, not through them. Only dark-skinned Australian natives live in these arid lands, and there are not many of them.

Those natives are as primitive as the Bushmen of Africa's Kalahari Desert. Perhaps if Australia had possessed native grain plants which could be cultivated, and native animals which could be domesticated, these people would have advanced toward civilization as men did in other continents of the world. But the Australian natives live today as men lived during the Stone Age.

They wear almost no clothes and decorate their bodies with scars and tattoo marks. They have no permanent homes, though they sometimes build temporary shelters out of grass, bark or branches as they move from place to place. They live on game and wild plants, and are skillful at finding water where none seems to exist. Their only domestic animal is a dog which Australians call a dingo.

The duty of the native woman is to gather edible roots, seeds and fruits, which she carries in a wooden bowl hacked out of gum wood. The duty of the man is to kill game. He is a remarkably good hunter even though his only weapon is a stone-tipped spear. He can catch snakes and lizards with his bare hands. He tracks down a kangaroo by running across the open desert in a brief spurt, freezing into stillness, and then running again, until at last he is close enough to hurl his spear for the kill.

The first white explorers of Australian deserts set out on their dangerous treks in the 1870s. They were looking for new lands that could be opened up to the continent's chief industry, cattle and sheep grazing. They learned that it was not even possible to drive cattle across those arid stretches from one coast to another. But now scientists are working their way slowly into the deserts in search of the kind of wealth already found on the deserts' edges—oil, gold, silver, copper, tin, lead, iron, tungsten and uranium. And if

Natives of the Australian deserts hunt kangaroos with spears.

riches are found under the central Australian desert floor, towns will almost certainly spring up there.

Water too may be found under that dry floor to support new settlements. Or if even deep well-digging operations prove useless, water may be brought into desert areas by some other means. Already one fairly new town, which has grown up near a rich desert iron deposit, receives water by a pipe line 223 miles long.

Modern industry may yet bring new life to the ancient Australian deserts that have so far remained unchanged for many thousands of years.

South America's Desert

South America's only desert, the Atacama, lies along the coast of northern Chile. Scientific records show that it is probably the driest place in the world. In certain areas the rainfall averages about half an inch a year, but often no rain falls there at all for many years at a time.

A man once wrote to English friends from the town of Iquique, at the edge of the desert, "If you are planning to visit me, don't bother to bring your umbrellas. I have lived here for fourteen years, and in all that time it has never rained once!"

Clifflike hills rise right out of the Pacific Ocean along the northern Chilean coast. Only at a few places is there room to squeeze a town in on the shore at the foot of the cliffs. Those towns very seldom get rain though moisture from the Pacific often wraps them in fog for days at a time.

Above the cliffs more gentle slopes continue to rise, to form a fairly high coastal range of mountains. Between the tops of those mountains and the tops of the Andes farther inland, is a broad shallow plateau-like valley. This valley, more than a mile above sea level, is the Atacama.

The Atacama is less than 100 miles wide, but it is more than 700 miles long. It begins at the northern tip of Chile and runs south as far as a town called Copiapó, capital of the Chilean province of Atacama. East of the desert, among the volcanic peaks of the high jagged Andes, is another desert-like area called the Puna de Atacama, which means "the bleak land of the Atacama." The Puna is also very dry, but often extremely cold.

In most places the Atacama is too dry to support any kind of life. Men who have explored it say they sometimes traveled forty miles across its brown and yellow rocks and sand without seeing a single blade of grass.

Almost no native Indians lived in the Atacama in the days before white men came to the New World.

The powerful Incas of Peru, who extended their empire south into what is now Bolívia and Chile, built a road down through the Atacama for the use of their conquering armies. But even the daring Incas didn't try to build towns in the desert.

The only Indian towns there today are located at the Atacama's few oases. Most of these are at very high altitudes, on mountains tall enough to trap an occasional rain cloud. Other oases are at the foot of hills, where water may collect underground. If the water is too far below the surface to be reached by plant roots, the Indians may dig away the whole top layer of soil. Then roots of the plants they sow can reach down to life-giving moisture.

The Indians plant forage crops for the herds of sheep they raise and for the llamas they use as pack animals. A llama cannot travel as fast as a mule travels and cannot carry very heavy loads, but he is a sturdy animal. His wool is valuable too. The Indians twist it into rope which can be sold for a high price. Mule drivers prefer it to any other kind for hobbling their animals at night. This is because the soft llama wool doesn't irritate a mule's skin.

Atacama Indians also plant trees called chañar trees,

In the Atacama Desert of Chile, the llama is a pack animal.

which bear nuts that look something like horse chest-
nuts. The hard white kernels are ground up and used
for soup and for the Indians' favorite food, chañar
bread.

Gold, silver and copper have all been found in the
Atacama, and the Spaniards mined those metals there
hundreds of years ago. Today the desert's most important product is nitrate, used in the making of fertilizers
and explosives.

When nitrate mining began in the Atacama, in about

the year 1880, several mining towns grew up there. Railroad lines were built from each town to the coast, and now all those towns are connected to each other by a railroad that runs the full length of the long narrow desert. Food and water and everything else the miners use must be brought into the mining towns by train or by mule packs.

Men in the hot arid mining towns sometimes ride the railroad tracks on a flat hand car fitted with a big sail. The sail catches the strong desert wind and moves them along at a rapid rate.

Antofagasta, on the coast, is the most important city in the Atacama region. It has a population of about 50,000.

This flat car is moved by the desert wind against the sail.

14

North America's Deserts

All the deserts of North America lie in two countries, the United States and Mexico.

A hundred years ago and more, when people drew maps of our continent, they usually put the words *Great American Desert* right across the entire western part of its great plains. This huge territory included the states of New Mexico, Arizona, Utah, Nevada, California, parts of Oregon, Colorado and Texas, and a great sweep of northern Mexico.

As more and more explorers crossed this vast region, however, they began to realize that not all of it was true desert. They found sections here and there that were not completely arid. They learned, in other words, that there was no single Great American Desert, but that there were several arid areas separated from each other by less dry territory. And on today's maps we read the names of those regions, which are now recognized as North America's major deserts. These are:

The Sonoran Desert of Arizona, extending south into Mexico

The Colorado Desert of California and Arizona

The Chihuahuan Desert, chiefly in Mexico but extending northward into Texas and New Mexico

The Mojave Desert of California, extending slightly into Nevada and Arizona

The Great Basin Desert of Utah and Nevada

Other smaller deserts also appear on our maps today, such as the desert of Vizcaino in Mexico's long peninsula of Lower California, and the dry plateau called the High Desert of Oregon. One of the most interesting of these smaller deserts is the Painted Desert in Arizona, with its terraces and mesas of red, yellow, purple and magenta sands. It includes the famous Petrified Forest, a wilderness of ancient tree trunks that have turned to stone.

Everywhere in the world low land is hotter than high land and is likely to be drier.

One of the hottest places in the world is Death Valley in the Mojave Desert. As you would expect, it is especially hot at the spot where it dips 282 feet below

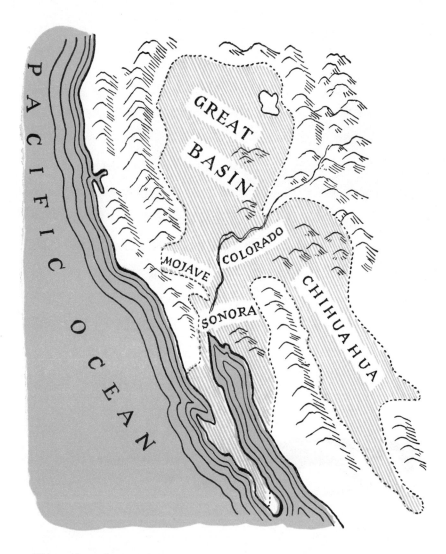

This map shows the five great deserts of North America.

sea level. If you climb one of the high mountains that form the valley itself, you move gradually into a cooler and probably moister climate. This is true of the high parts of every desert valley.

If you were to climb up such a mountain, you would

move into cooler and cooler zones of climate. And you would find the plant and animal life around you changing with each zone.

At the very foot of the mountain, close to sea level, you would see leafless cacti and the animals that are able to endure the most heat and dryness.

As you made your way up the lower slope, the cactus plants would begin to disappear. In their place you might see ocotillo and creosote bushes, making shelter and patches of scant shade for lizards and kangaroo rats.

The lizard is found up high where cactus is disappearing.

By the time you had reached the altitude of 3,500 feet, you would be at the level where sagebrush, stunted juniper trees and piñon pines grow. The lizards and snakes would be different from the ones you had seen in the lower zone. There might be prairie dogs, too, and long-eared black-tailed jack rabbits.

The long-eared jack rabbit and prairie dog are found still higher.

Farther up, at about 7,000 feet above sea level, you would enter still another "life zone," as scientists call these different levels of altitude. Here you might see ponderosa pines alive with birds, swift-moving chipmunks and perhaps a mountain lion.

If you climbed high enough, over 12,000 feet above sea level, you would be in a life zone so cold that it can support only tough grass and lichens. There you might even find yourself surrounded by snow and ice. Yet far below you might still be able to see an arid desert floor baked by a temperature hotter than 100 degrees.

Scientists have divided North American desert country into seven of these life zones. Here is a list of them, giving the scientific name for each, its altitude, its rainfall, and the type of country where it can be found:

All About the Desert

Life Zone	Feet Above Sea Level	Inches of Rain Each Year	Where Found
Arctic-Alpine	above 12,000	30–35	Above timber line
Hudsonian	9,500–12,000	30–35	High mountains to timber line
Canadian	8,000–10,000	25–30	Mountains
Transition	7,000–8,000	19–25	Plateau lands
Upper Sonoran	3,500–7,000	12–20	Mesas and foothills and Great Basin Desert
Lower Sonoran	500–4,000	3–15	Sonoran, Mojave and Chihuahuan deserts
Dry Tropical	below 500	1–6	Along Colorado River in extreme southwest Arizona

Some of the zone names, such as Arctic-Alpine and Canadian, tell us right away what kind of climate that zone has. Some of them, especially Lower and Upper Sonoran, are more confusing. The word Sonoran was used first as the name of a state in northern Mexico. Then it was used for the name of the desert that covers most of that Mexican region and part of Arizona too. Then it was used again in the names of two life zones, because both these zones are found in the Sonoran Desert. But it is important to remember that the names

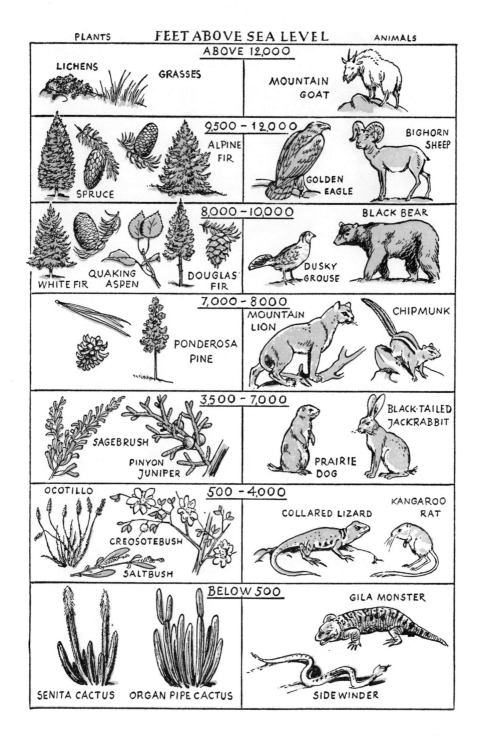

ABOVE 12,000

LICHENS   GRASSES   MOUNTAIN GOAT

9,500 – 12,000

ALPINE FIR   SPRUCE   GOLDEN EAGLE   BIGHORN SHEEP

8,000 – 10,000

WHITE FIR   QUAKING ASPEN   DOUGLAS FIR   DUSKY GROUSE   BLACK BEAR

7,000 – 8,000

PONDEROSA PINE   MOUNTAIN LION   CHIPMUNK

3,500 – 7,000

SAGEBRUSH   PINYON JUNIPER   PRAIRIE DOG   BLACK-TAILED JACKRABBIT

500 – 4,000

OCOTILLO   CREOSOTEBUSH   SALTBUSH   COLLARED LIZARD   KANGAROO RAT

BELOW 500

SENITA CACTUS   ORGAN PIPE CACTUS   GILA MONSTER   SIDEWINDER

All About the Desert

Lower Sonoran Zone and Upper Sonoran Zone do not refer to any particular desert, but to a particular kind of climate and to the plants and animals that live in that climate.

Most of the land in our North American deserts lies in these two zones. Some deserts lie partly in one and partly in the other, and they may be dotted with mesas and mountains that reach high into some of the upper life zones.

These sharp ups and downs, with their different life zones lying so close together, make our North American desert region one of the most fascinating areas in our continent.

As the chart shows, the plant and animal life in each of our separate deserts depends largely on the zone that desert is in. In other words, Lower Sonoran zones all look quite a lot alike, because they have the same kinds of plants and animals. This is true whether they are in the Sonoran, the Mojave or the Chihuahuan Deserts.

Plants That Point

If you are riding westward toward the Chihuahuan Desert, you can be sure you have arrived when you see one particular plant—the agave. This has stiff pointed

The stiff pointed leaves of the agave grow in a low circle.

green leaves growing in a circle close to the ground. The country around may not look much drier than the country you have just passed, but the presence of the agave is a sure sign that this is the Chihuahuan Desert. Scientists say this plant indicates or points out, at least roughly, the boundaries of that desert. They call it the "indicator plant" of the Chihuahuan.

When the agave plant is about fifteen years old or older, it sends up a single tall stalk tipped with a cluster of yellow flowers. Many people think the agave blooms only after a hundred years of growth. For that reason, it is sometimes called the century plant.

All About the Desert

Indians have always used this plant in many ways, and Mexicans cultivate it today in large fields because it is so useful. They thatch their roofs with its leaves, make rope and a coarse cloth from the leaf fiber, and make several different drinks from its juice. The Mexican name for the agave is *maguey* (mah-GAY-e).

Other deserts have indicator plants too.

In the Mojave Desert it is the Joshua tree. It was given its odd name more than a century ago by Mormon pioneers traveling through the desert. When they saw it outlined against the sky, they thought it looked like a man raising his arms to lead them on their way. So they named it in honor of the prophet Joshua in the Bible, who led his people into the Promised Land of Jordan.

Wood rats, birds and small lizards make their homes in the shade of the Joshua tree or in its shaggy branches. At the tip of those branches are the plant's white flowers, growing in big clusters.

The Joshua tree, like other members of the yucca family, is interesting for a special reason. When it is in bloom, a certain kind of moth lays her eggs in the tube-like pistil of the flower, and then presses down on top of the eggs a small ball of pollen collected from other yucca flowers. Yuccas couldn't reproduce themselves if

White flowers bloom at the tips of the Joshua tree's branches.

the moth didn't bring them that pollen from other plants, which fertilizes the yuccas' seeds. And the larvae that hatch out of the moth eggs couldn't survive without the pollen and some of the plant's seeds to eat. This is one of the most curious examples known to scientists of plant life and animal life depending on each other.

For a time it seemed that all Joshua trees might some-day disappear because they were growing fewer each year. But now a large Joshua tree forest in the Mojave Desert has become a national monument. This means that it has been taken over by the United States government to be protected and preserved for all people to see and enjoy.

The treelike saguaro cactus is the indicator plant of the Sonoran Desert. This tallest of all members of the cactus family is sometimes called the giant cactus. It has a thick main stalk, or trunk, and upward branching arms that may rise to more than three times the height of a man. It can store an enormous amount of water in its accordion-pleated stalks and survive severe drought to live for as long as 200 years.

The saguaro's waxy white flowers, which bloom at the tips of its stalks, are followed by fruits that look like little egg-shaped cucumbers. They are a deep red inside, filled with tiny black seeds, and are very good to eat.

National monuments have also been set up to protect a forest of saguaro cactus and a forest of that other big cactus, the organ pipe cactus, whose tall stalks rise straight up like the pipes of some huge outdoor organ. These forests, both in the Sonoran Desert, attract thousands of visitors each year. This is because they are really big wild gardens of many different kinds of desert plants, and natural zoos where lizards, snakes, birds and many other forms of desert wild life may be seen.

In the spring tiny blossoms appear on the organ pipe cactus.

The Saguaro National Monument and the Organ Pipe Cactus National Monument are especially popular in the spring because that's when the cacti bloom. And that's when thousands of small short-lived plants spring up everywhere beneath them. Then, almost overnight, the whole bare desert floor is briefly carpeted with thousands of delicate little flowers in almost every color of the rainbow—pink, yellow, red, orange, blue and lavender.

Some people dislike desert plants because they fear their many spines or thorns. Others say desert plants are the most beautiful in the world. But everyone who has ever visited our American deserts knows that there is a special excitement in the first sight of an agave plant or a Joshua tree or a tall saguaro. The sight of one of those plants is a signal. It means that the visitor can say, "Look! The first one! We have reached the desert."

They Came First

The first Indians to see our American deserts were primitive hunters, members of many different tribes that long ago wandered over this wild and empty land.

In the beginning they probably had no homes at all or lived in caves. But gradually they began to build primitive houses by digging holes in the ground and covering them over. Their tools were primitive too. To add to their diet of wild roots and fruits and berries, they killed game by hurling small spears or darts. But they made sandals out of woven yucca fiber and wove robes out of strips of rabbit skin for cold weather. And they became very skillful at weaving fine tight baskets out of roots and stems and fibers. That's why they have been called the Basketmakers.

The next inhabitants of our deserts probably came into that area from somewhere farther south about 1,200 years ago. These were the Pueblo Indians, and they either conquered the Basketmakers or joined forces with them. They too were people of many different tribes, but the name used for all of them together tells us that they all lived in pueblos or villages. They were able to settle down, instead of wandering around in search of game, because they had developed agriculture. They planted beans and corn and cotton and kept flocks of domesticated turkeys. Dogs were their only other domesticated animals. The Pueblos too made baskets, but usually they stored their food in fine pottery jars or bowls. Today Pueblo Indians are still famous for their excellent pottery.

Probably most of the Pueblos orginally settled down at places where water was easy to obtain, near springs or along rivers. But we know that many of them dug wells, and we know that the Pueblo people called Hohokam, the Canal Builders, brought water to their villages by a network of canals.

At first the Pueblos built houses as the Basketmakers did, by digging pits and roofing them over. But soon they began to raise their roofs higher and to support them by walls of stone or packed mud. Finally the pit became only a small storage compartment in the floor of a square house built around it.

Sometimes they piled these one-room houses on top

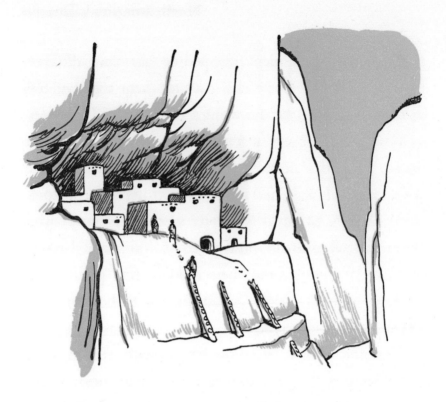

Pueblo Indians often built adobe houses in caves.

of each other to form a terraced structure large enough
to hold an entire village. They reached the upper rooms
by ladders and lived safely inside the inner rooms, using
the lower and outer ones for storage only.

Sometimes they built these stone or adobe houses inside a huge natural cave in the side of a tall cliff. In some
cases there were so many one-room houses piled on top
of each other inside the cave that the cave was almost
entirely filled. Usually these cliff dwellings could be

reached only by ladders propped against the cliff from the valley below. If the cliff dwellers kept their ladders in the cave, they were always safe from their enemies.

The center of every Pueblo village was a real pit house, a circular hole so deep that its roof was level with the ground. It had to be entered by a ladder from above. This structure, called a *kiva*, was the place where all sacred rituals and ceremonies of the village took place.

Many Indians of our Southwest, who now live on Indian reservations scattered through several states, still build pueblos much like those their ancestors used. And in our deserts may also be seen the remains of ancient pueblos which are being preserved as national monuments.

Casa Grande National Monument in the Sonoran Desert, for example, is the ruins of an ancient Hohokam walled city, built more than 800 years ago. A four-story adobe tower, probably used as a watchtower, stood in the center of the town. Father Eusebio Francisco Kino, the Jesuit missionary who was the first white man to see this place, called the tower Casa Grande, which is Spanish for "big house." People today call it America's first skyscraper.

All About the Desert

Montezuma Castle National Monument, also in the Sonoran Desert, is one of the best preserved of all known ancient Indian cliff dwellings. This five-story pink adobe castle, built inside a high cave, was given its name by early white explorers. They believed that Montezuma, the great Aztec chief of Mexico, had once lived here. But no one today really knows which Indian tribe built this long-abandoned place.

The Newcomer

Spanish explorers, like the trail-blazing Franciscan priest, Marcos de Niza, were the first white men to see our American deserts. They came north from Mexico, along a trail they called the Journey of Death, to search for new wealth and new rich lands to add to the glory of Spain's New World colony. Soon they laid claim to what they called the Province of New Mexico. This extended from the Mississippi River to the Pacific Coast and northward from the Mexico boundary as far as any white men had traveled.

Those first Spaniards found very little of the kind of wealth they were seeking—gold and silver and jewels—and most of the treasure seekers soon departed. The two groups of Spaniards who remained to settle in this largely arid region were cattle raisers and priests.

The cattle raisers built fine ranches and grazed their animals over thousands of acres of land. The priests built missions, taught the friendly Pueblo Indians to grow new grains and vegetables, introduced them for the first time to horses and cows, and tried to convert them to Christianity.

Many Indians were willing to adopt the new ways of life brought by the white men. They became Christians, even though they didn't give up the rituals and ceremonies of their own religion. Thousands moved from their own pueblos to live in large communities around missions like the Church of San José de Tumacacori, which still stands near the big modern city of Tucson.

But the more warlike tribes began to raid the missions, to steal herds and food and to destroy churches. This was in revenge against the Spaniards who had seized their land and the Indians who had become the Spaniards' allies.

The trouble between white men and Indians was not settled even when Mexico, including the old province of New Mexico, gained its freedom from Spain. Indian raids and massacres were still fairly common when the next group of newcomers arrived. These were American explorers, prospectors and pioneers who had traveled westward from beyond the Mississippi.

All About the Desert

Some of those Americans reached this region before it became part of the United States at the end of the Mexican War in 1848. After that war the stream of new arrivals grew heavier. Not all of the westward-traveling Americans settled in the desert to become miners or cattlemen. A good many of them were just passing through on their way to the gold fields and the new farm land being opened up in California. Even those who didn't stop, however, needed to purchase fresh supplies on their way. So trading posts were soon set up to serve them.

Those trading posts, along the routes used by pioneer wagon trains, gave birth to new desert towns. So did the opening up of new silver, gold and copper mines. Some of those early American settlements became ghost towns long ago. Others are still thriving today.

One other kind of newcomer reached our desert areas during the same period that brought so many prospectors there. These people were not seeking wealth. They were Mormons, seeking the religious freedom they hadn't been able to find in their original home in New York state.

Moving slowly westward, the Mormons were persecuted wherever they tried to settle. Finally they decided that they would find real freedom only in a land so barren that nobody else lived in it or would ever want to live in it. When they looked down from a mountain top at the desert surrounding Great Salt Lake, they said, "This is the place." There, in 1847, they founded Salt Lake City and immediately began to plow and irrigate the gray desert floor. Today thousands of acres of the Great Salt Lake Desert, which is part of the Great Basin Desert, have been transformed into good farm land by members of the Mormon Church.

Newly irrigated land is attracting still more farmers to our Southwest today, and there is a new wave of prospectors too. These late-coming prospectors don't bend over a stream to pan gravel, in the hope of finding flecks of gold. Few of them travel with the old prospector's faithful friend, the burro. Instead they bounce across the desert in jeeps or fly over it in planes. They use sensitive instruments to detect the presence of uranium or some other valuable metal, or perhaps a hidden source of oil, far beneath the desert floor.

But today there are many newcomers arriving in our American deserts for reasons that are different from the reasons that brought people there in the past.

One group consists of scientists who find there the best possible conditions for certain experiments: clear air, year-round warm weather and sunshine, and emptiness. With these conditions they can conduct outdoors tests at any time, knowing they can count on unlimited visibility and certain that no human beings will be near enough to be injured by their explosions or their long-range projectiles.

That's why the world's first atomic bomb, for example, was set off in the Chihuahuan Desert in 1945. And that's why experimental rockets have been fired in that same desert ever since the first testing station was set up in 1930.

Few outsiders are ever permitted inside the government's rocket-testing station in the desert today, but anyone can see the kind of country the scientists prefer by visiting the nearby White Sands National Monument. This is a great expanse of dunes formed of gleaming white gypsum, a powdery substance sometimes used in making building materials, cleaners and fertilizers. But it is almost useless for supporting any kind of life. Here almost nothing grows except a few yuccas, which can thrust their roots down a dozen yards to find the life-giving water beneath this dead dryness. Here nothing lives, to be injured by explosions, except a few mice, beetles and insects, all as white—or nearly as white—as the gypsum sands themselves.

Another group of recent desert newcomers are tourists. They come from all parts of the world, more of them every year, to see and experience the many wonders, man-made and natural, that exist in our American deserts.

They watch people at work, in ways that are as new as tomorrow—operating big modern irrigation systems, farming recently irrigated land, smelting copper by large-scale modern methods.

They see how people used to live and work by visiting ghost towns, abandoned Indian villages, and places that have changed very little for many years. At Tombstone, Arizona, for example, they can walk along streets that still look just as they did in the 1880s, when the town was boisterously rich on the silver dug from the Tombstone, the Lucky Cuss and the Tough Nut mines. At the Papago Indian Reservation in the Sonoran Desert, they can talk with families living in mud-floored huts built of mud-plastered cactus ribs and ocotillo stems, and grinding mesquite beans into meal just as their ancestors did long ago.

They see famous sights that have been described in hundreds of books—weird rock formations, fantastic canyons and gorges, the strange outpouring of bats each dusk

Each evening swarms of bats come from Carlsbad caverns.

from one of the caves of the Carlsbad Caverns, the automobile race course near Great Salt Lake that is really a stretch of natural salt one hundred miles long.

And the tourists who come to look and wonder can also, if they choose, stand alone at the edge of an empty stretch of desert and imagine that no man has ever seen that place before. Like the first desert explorer, they can look toward the far horizon and see no sign of human life, can listen in the utter silence and hear no sound.

For some people this is one of our deserts' greatest attractions. There they feel that they can see, as they could see almost nowhere else, a land that has never changed, a land that looks as if it would never change for as long as it lies hot and dry under the blazing desert sun.

15

Tomorrow's Deserts

One of the most important questions being asked in the world today is this: Will science finally transform all deserts into fertile fields? Can farms and cities thrive in every area where nothing now exists except sun-baked sand and stone?

Nobody can be sure of the answer to that question, but it seems likely that the answer is no.

In fact, many scientists say that the world's desert areas are growing drier all the time. They remind us that the Kalahari had flowing rivers and streams only several hundred years ago. They remind us, too, that only 2,000 years ago—which is not a very long time, in the history of the world—lions and elephants were being captured in forest lands in what is now the northern Sahara. Today, of course, such animals couldn't exist in the Sahara. Today there are no forests in that region because it is too dry.

How do scientists explain this drying up of certain regions? Again there is no certain answer to that question. Some think it is caused by a great slow change that has long been taking place in the earth's climate, and that is still going on, causing a decrease in rainfall and therefore an increase in desert areas.

Scientists also think that man himself had something to do with the creation or growth of desert areas. Man, they say, cut down forests and over-cultivated fields so that once fertile soil could no longer hold, or make use of, the rainfall it received. Then that soil was on its way to becoming a desert. We do know, for example, that the over-cultivation of soil, and the soil erosion that followed it, made a "dust bowl" out of a vast region in the United States within only a few short years. Millions of trees and thousands of acres of tough grass are being planted in that region now in an attempt to bring it back to its once fertile state.

A new question has recently been added to the great question about the future of our deserts. It is this: Can we continue to increase indefinitely the number of irrigation pumps now taking water up from far beneath the desert floor?

The answer to that question is almost certainly no. Already the water table, as scientists call this underground water supply, is dropping alarmingly. French engineers report, for example, that when they pump an unusually large amount of water out of certain Sahara wells, the water level in wells some distance away falls sharply.

We are learning, in other words, that the supply of underground water beneath our deserts cannot be pumped up, year after year, at a rate much faster than it collects there.

It is possible that new methods for bringing water to our deserts may be developed in the future.

Engineers have suggested that a great canal might be cut through the mountains lying between the Mediterranean Sea and the Sahara, so that an inland sea might be created in a low portion of that desert. It would be a salt sea, of course, and useless for irrigation purposes. But the men who have suggested this scheme think that clouds will form over that sea, as the hot sun sucks up the water, and that those clouds will bring rain to the desert at the sea's edge.

All About the Desert

Scientists are also working hard to develop large-scale methods for removing salt and minerals from sea water. Present-day methods for doing this are far too expensive to be practical for use in big irrigation systems. But some day, perhaps by the use of atomic energy or by some chemical method, the world's oceans may become sources of huge amounts of fresh water for the world's deserts.

Man may be careful to prevent now-green areas from becoming arid. He may build new inland seas inside some deserts and irrigate others with ocean water turned fresh. But probably even then there will always be desert areas somewhere in the world.

Would we want them all to disappear? Probably the answer to that question is a very definite no. Probably most people would say that at least some deserts should always be preserved. Then the men of the future, like the men of the past, can marvel at their wonders and seek to unlock their secrets.

Index

Index

Index